SECRETS OF A SE

COACH

BY IVAN IVOVIC

ISBN 978-1-105-02033-9

Secrets of a Serbian Water Polo Coach:

Table of Contents

INTRODUCTION

As a coach I am always looking for what's new in water polo coaching world, so I thought this time I would go ahead and share some knowledge and in this way give my part to this beautiful sport. This book is not about drills that will improve the game of your team, but about specific tactics you can use to solve problems during a game. The manual serves as a tool to learn and later refer to real game solutions that occur during a match. Therefore, it is not meant to provide the practice drills for every situation that I explain. It is up to coaches and players to come up with the practice drills in order to gain a specific skill. After all, when you see a final product of how the play should look like, you should be able to break it down into breakable pieces and teach the players how to do it.

In order to refine the game of water polo, as coaches we dissect each tactic into its' smallest parts, and we practice those first, later connecting them into bigger pieces, and finally fitting them into a cohesive whole. It is like practicing piano. When you want to master a piece of music, you first practice the left hand, then the right hand. After this is perfect, you put the two parts together and practicing each bar repeatedly. When this has been perfected, you string all of the bars together and can confidently play a beautiful piece of music. All of these elements apply to my water polo coaching style. I expect my athletes to be perfect at each minute detail of the game and I inspire them to master all of the elements until they are moving like clockwork through the water.

NOTES ON THE TEXT

Every coach has his or her own language for players that she coaches. For example: some coaches use the term "tips" to describe the passing drill of touching the ball with the tips of your fingers, whereas other coaches use the term "taps" to describe the same drill.

Throughout this book, I have used terms in the way we use them in my native language – Serbian. Some of these terms may not be familiar to US water polo coaches, or coaches from different regions. I have included a glossary at the end of the text to fully explain each term. I'm not trying to change the name of a certain action or play; I simply want the reader to be exposed to another water polo language.

Throughout this book, I have broken new ground by using the pronoun "she" to represent the player. This isn't meant to be sexist or exclusionist; just meant to be expeditious for the reader and I thought girls that play water polo finally should have a manual that refers primarily to them.

NOTES ON THE ILLUSTRATIONS

Introduction: throughout this book I showed drawings in the exact way a certain action should go, but the point is that water polo is a free flowing sport and should not be set in stone in terms of steps during tactics. It is an art and many solutions are possible. The reason I provided the drawings and exact steps is to give idea to the readers on one possibility of how a certain play can be done and not to say that my way is the only way. Though, when I coach, I make sure my players realize that it's my way or the highway...

I've included a legend for each illustration that provides a key to what each element of the play means. I urge you to refer back to this, as some of the drawings are complex and have a lot going on – much like the game of water polo!

When I describe the offensive tactics, the numbering starts on the viewer's right side of each illustration; i.e., player #1 is typically in the upper right corner, wrapping around like a semi-circle until we get to #5 in the left corner, with the hole-man, #6, in the center. This isn't always the case for the defense. When you have even numbers of players, the defense will start the same way as offense; Player #1 is in the top right corner. However, during the man-down situations, player #1 is in the top left corner, with the other players arrayed counterclockwise – so in the opposite manner as the offense.

It's important to note that the player's numbers in the figures are not always fixed, especially in man-down situations. That is to say player #3 on offense – going back to defense – can sometimes pop into player #5's spot and actually become player #5 in my figure. This can be confusing if you don't read the text above each figure. I have explained the action so that the figure is meant to be a pictorial display of my words; without the accompanying text, it might be easy to get lost in the figures.

I am including a legend so that you can easily understand the figures I've created. Please familiarize yourself with these icons and refer back to it as needed.

Legend:

- ② - player on offense
- ❷ - player on defense
- ❷⌐ - player blocking shot
- ↰ - movement of a player
- * - ending position of a player
- ↖ - pass
- ↖ - shot
- o - ball
- ⌡ - pick
- ⌡ - swim around

Also, in Serbia and Montenegro, the white players are the offensive players, and the black the defensive. I realize that this isn't the case for American water polo so please keep this in mind when studying the figures. In Serbia and Montenegro, the home team always wears white caps and the away team wears the dark colored caps. This doesn't really matter for the illustrations, but I thought I'd share a little trivia for when you're watching our awesome Serbian or Montenegrin National teams play!

This book is written from a coaches' perspective, but it's not solely for coaches. It is designed to be easy to understand for anyone who wants to get into the game.

So how is this book for players? By studying the tactics in this book, players will be one step ahead of other players because when their coach introduces the concepts I've covered, they will be prepared and know what to expect – that will give them a competitive edge against the competition.

And parents of players and fans of the sport? Once you understand what is actually happening in the water, and go deeper than just the basics, you will enjoy watching the game much more. When you recognize that your daughter, son or friend just broke the zone defense you will keep coming back for more!

ABOUT THE AUTHOR

A lot of my life was spent preparing to write this book. If you know anything about the sport of water polo, you know that the Yugoslavia National Men's Water Polo team – is one of the most successful water polo teams in the history of the sport. We have a proud heritage, and when you look at the roster of the college teams that lead the field here in the United States, you can see a smattering of names that come from former Yugoslavia.

I come from a water polo family – it's in my blood. I have a cousin who currently plays for the Montenegrin National Men's Water Polo team, who won the European Championship in 2008. My father and my uncle both played the sport growing up in Montenegro. On the streets of the little town where they grew up, I heard that my father was one of the best penalty shooter in his day, and that my uncle was fast and had a flutter kick like a torpedo. He was so good that he played for the first league team in Montenegro in former Yugoslavia. Of course, I always wanted to follow in their footsteps.

My father was an avid athlete through his college years, but once he moved to Belgrade to work and start a family, he did not have the time that he would have liked to have spent playing water polo – so he encouraged me from the minute I expressed interest. Though we lived in Belgrade during the school year, as far back as I can remember we would spend every summer at the seaside in Montenegro, where my family has a house right next to the pool in the sea itself. Naturally, there were constant matches popping up, and as soon as I was able to swim, I was playing for the local team, *Rivijera Djenovici.*

During the school year when I was back in Belgrade, I was a competitive swimmer – since I was 7, from September to June I was going to daily practices, often taking the bus for an hour before dawn to swim before the school bell rang. Because I was swimming all year round, I was able to play as one of the starters on *Rivijera Djenovici* from a young age.

While I was a student at the University of Belgrade, Faculty of Sport and Physical Education, studying to be a Physical Education instructor, I learned that there was an opportunity to simultaneously get my degree in Water Polo Coaching. Naturally, I was excited about this chance to gain a deeper understanding of the sport. Soon after I completed my degree, I moved to the Washington, DC metro area and started playing for a local club team and coaching at Gonzaga College High School, a private Catholic boy's school. I finished my undergrad at the University of Maryland, where I played on the men's club team while I was getting my degree in Kinesiology. I graduated *summa cum laude* with high honors from the program, even though I was busy coaching the high school team, and celebrated the birth of my daughter 6 months prior.

Realizing my high school athletes needed more playing time to really excel, I started a club team for them to practice during off season a few years ago, and we have seen tremendous progress since then. The interest from the Gonzaga students has doubled in the years I have been with the program, and now we have 50 kids and 4 JV and Varsity teams that compete nearly every weekend in the Fall.

ACKNOWLEDGEMENTS

I would specifically like to thank my instructor, Zoran Bratusa, MS, who was my mentor at the University of Belgrade, Faculty of Water Polo in Belgrade, Serbia. He provided me with the tools it takes to be a successful coach, and he himself was a great water polo player who still coaches and prepares new coaches in Belgrade.

A special thank you to Joe Viola, who took a chance on me even though I was "fresh off the boat" and though degreed, had no formal experience coaching. Together we make a great team, and he has taught me a lot about what being a coach in the United States really means.

The student athletes with whom I have had the pleasure to spend the last several years have really contributed to my success as a coach, and several of them are currently playing at the college level. Whenever I have an opportunity to see them play, I recognize skills that I taught them and I am proud to have contributed to their success as well.

I also want to thank my wife, Tina, who has been patient and ready to listen when I was telling her about upcoming matches and whose love was always supporting me at whatever I was doing.

PHOTOGRAPH 1: BOY'S VARSITY TEAM, GONZAGA COLLEGE HIGH SCHOOL, 2011

PHOTOGRAPH 2: BOY'S JUNIOR VARSITY TEAM, GONZAGA COLLEGE HIGH SCHOOL, 2011

SECRETS OF A SERBIAN WATER POLO COACH

This manual is a tool for players, coaches and ambitious parents who want to gain a deeper understanding of the game. It came as a product of me playing, watching, studying, coaching and living in a water polo family in a country that is the cradle of the sport of water polo.

Like every novel has a main character, this book also has a protagonist, and that person is the Top Driver/Center Defender. The point of view you will most often see the game through is that of the top driver.

I thought that the best way to start this book is to say that the three most important positions on any given water polo team are the top driver (position #3), the center/hole-man (position #6) and the goalie. These three positions are often called the framework of the team. If a team has good players in these positions it is more likely that the team will achieve greater results. This does not mean that the other four positions are not important and that players should get discouraged if they don't play on these positions. It just serves as information to the reading audience that the game is usually built around these three players. I always like to have a player from one of these positions as the captain of my team.

The figure below illustrates the numbers and names I will be using to describe the players when they are on offense and defense.

> *...the three most important positions on any given water polo team are the top driver (position #3), the center/hole-man (position #6) and the goalie.*

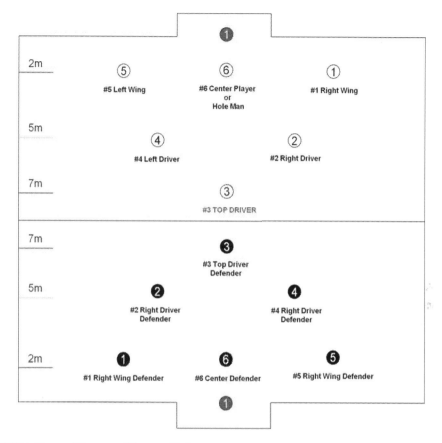

FIGURE 1: Names of Players on Offense and Defense

In the text when I'm describing player #3 during offense, I will refer to her as the Top Driver, and when I'm talking about her on defense I will refer to her as the "center-defender" or as a "hole-defender".

One could argue that the top driver/hole defender is the most important player on the team. To perform in this position, the athlete must be very active on offense and defense. Because of her unique position on offense, she has the best view of the entire field, so she is in the best position to be the "playmaker" of the team. Also, she is the first to swim back on defense, and is the last line on defense nearest the goal. No other player has the same advantage on both offense and defense.

Experienced coaches know that it's essential to build your team around your defenders, so you can prevent other teams from scoring on you. That is why when I select players for my team, I pick ones who can prevent the goal over those who can score, any day of the week. The benefits are twofold; a strong defense builds confidence in all of your players, and wears down the morale of the opposing team.

I am a defense kind of coach, and this is why. Once you teach your team to play an impenetrable defense, you have control over the game. If you can build mastery of this more subtle aspect of the game – the defense – your team will be stronger and more disciplined. Every new player is anxious to start scoring goals immediately, but if you break them down by forcing them to hold back from shooting and make them practice the defensive tactics rigorously, they will remember these lessons for the rest of their lives, and perhaps even transfer that discipline over to other aspects of their lives. In Serbia, it's typical for athletes to return to their coaches and thank them for all of the life lessons they learned as athletes under their care.

Understanding the game played by the top driver will enhance the water polo IQ of every player, no matter what position she plays. It will also help see the whole game through a different lens, which is one of the goals of this book. In the next section, I will describe the top driver/center defender position and further delve into every aspect of her game.

In the majority of this book, I will present different tactics for playing water polo, but in order for players to be able to accomplish these maneuvers they need to have technical skills. Many of your players will have varying degrees of skill in these areas, but as coach, your mission is to fully develop their potential and create a team with uniformly excellent skills. This is something that I strive for in my athletes, and why we train as hard as we do. While I understand that it may not be possible to get everyone to play at the same level, the saying, "the team is only as good as it's weakest link" rings true and gives us motivation to have everyone bring it to the next level. Believe me, it takes discipline and commitment from all involved to work toward that goal. But the results will be worth the effort.

TECHNICAL SKILLS

> *...when I select players for my team, I pick ones who can prevent the goal over those who can score, any day of the week.*

Before you can play water polo at even the most basic level, you need to have a pretty basic set of skills. You can't build the first story of a house if you don't have a foundation built first. These technical skills are the basis of what you will use during practice – you must know how to handle the ball, you must know how to fake, you must know how to get open from a defender – before you can compete against another team.

This is not meant to be an in-depth study of these techniques. The reason why I won't go deep into the techniques necessary to play water polo is because video explanations and coaches' instructions from the pool deck are always superior to the written word. On the other hand, tactics are a different animal and can be successfully explained through text. There are several more thorough examples out there in the water polo literature, but I thought it would be a good idea to start with these as building blocks for our tactical sections.

THE TECHNIQUE OF CATCHING AND THROWING THE BALL

Every player, including the top driver, needs to perfect the art of catching and throwing the ball. This means that she needs to be able to catch and throw the ball to her teammate with ease. In order to do this the player has to:

1. **Have a high vertical position in the water**, which is a product of good eggbeater technique and strong/conditioned legs. The eggbeater skill is the most important technique in the game of water polo. It is used in every situation and players have to be able to tread water - at the highest level of competition – for hours straight. Different drills can help this skill develop; treading with the hands out, treading with the arms out, treading while holding an object above the head, and treading while moving in different directions.

2. **Be able to pass the ball precisely**, with little or no spin. If the ball has spin, it should have a bottom spin so that the teammate can catch the ball without the ball rolling out of the hand. A bottom spin is created when the ball is passed over the middle finger, which was the last point of contact with the ball.

3. **Be able to control the ball** that's in the hand. This comes with time and practice. Some players have a great feeling for the ball and are ambidextrous, and some practice catching and throwing a lot and still are stiff. My advice is to take catching and throwing drills during practice very seriously, and take the time to practice by juggling and doing other passing and catching games on dryland with different kinds of balls. It's also worth mentioning that players should practice passing with both the left and the right hand. What we see happening in modern water polo is that players are using both hands in order to pass the ball or shoot from close distances.

THE TECHNIQUE OF FAKING (ALSO KNOWN AS PUMPING)

In my opinion, besides eggbeater and passing, the faking technique comes in a strong third. The goal for each offense is to take a high percentage shot, and that shot usually should come after a fake. Having a good technique of faking is therefore important because enables the player to throw the goalie and the defense out of balance and have a better chance of scoring or setting up one of her teammates for the shot. The best fakes should be disguised so that every fake you make looks like you're going to release the ball, but then you bring it back again and you shoot on the next move. The fake should look the same for lob shot, skip shot, pass, hesitation shot or any other kind of shot.

THE TECHNIQUE OF GETTING OPEN

In order for top driver (player #3) to be dangerous and actively participate on offense she needs to be able to easily get separated from the defender. There is always a weak link in the defense and if it happens to be at the top driver position, the top driver has to use that to her advantage and use "one on one" tactics. If this happens to be the case, then the top driver can break free and drive forward and her defender (player #3) won't be able to follow her, which will allow an opportunity to score. Before the shot is finally taken, the goal is to always have an advantage in relation to the other player in at least one of the positions. In other words, one of the players has to beat her opponent in order for a shot to be taken. This advantage can be such that the player on offense is in front of her defender (the player has gotten inside water advantage by driving) or that the defender is not blocking the correct part of the goal effectively either by being too far back (double teaming the center) or too far to the side. These techniques typically are used when the defense is playing a pressure defense and it is hard to move the ball around. The more we move the ball around, the more we move the defense and the goalie, and the more likely we are to break the pressure defense and score. In order for the top driver to get open she can do several things:

THE REAR BACK (RB) TECHNIQUE: This technique consists of a player driving toward the goal and suddenly changing direction by throwing herself on her back. The defender will not know when the player is going to change direction and will continue swimming towards the cage. This late realization will result in a player getting open. In order to get open by driving and by doing the RB, the player needs to have a strong and explosive start. This requires strong legs and very efficient egg beater and scissors kick techniques. After an explosive start the player who is driving has to have her elbows up high and has to be making short strokes so that in case she is being held the referee can easily spot this and kick the other player out. High frequency short strokes, rather than long strokes, provide better acceleration in swimming. This is similar to other cyclical sports, such as running, cycling, and rowing. This drive lasts only for 1-2 meters and is followed by a strong scissors kick and the RB. This is how we get the space we need to get the ball to the open player so that she can shoot, fake or pass (triple threat situation) to the player who in the meantime got open as well. The element of surprise is crucial here, the drive needs to happen suddenly and without expectation (with a "poker face" so to speak).

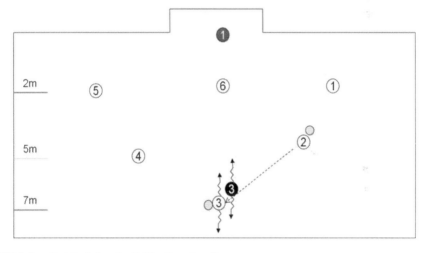

FIGURE 2: Rear Back Technique for Getting Open for a Pass

RB WITHOUT THE DRIVE FORWARD: This is when the player throws herself on her back suddenly, but she hasn't gone forward prior; instead she has taken a couple of backstrokes, or she has jumped to one side – sort of like a goalie jump – in order to get open.

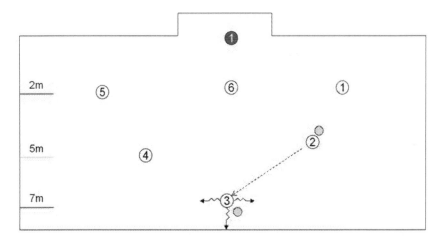

FIGURE 3: RB without the Drive Forward

BACK DOOR DRIVE: This is when the player simply drives toward one of the posts, stops at the 2 meter line and does a high jump. At that very moment the player is passed the ball by her teammate and she can make an easy score. I use this drill for a warm up at almost every practice; it has elements of a man-on-man duel, it has sprint swimming elements, and shooting elements.

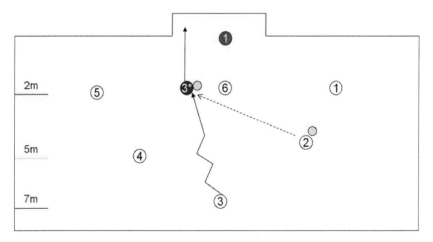

FIGURE 4: Back Door Drive

Usually when the driver is beating the defender she should make the high jump at 2 meter line expecting the pass, and taking advantage of the inside water she is inside of, instead of doing the RB, which is utilized when the defender is hard to get by, or there isn't enough space to get in front of her.

20

TACTICS DURING DEFENSE AND OFFENSE

Top Driver Tactics During Defense

You could say that the tactics of the top driver/center-defender (known in this section solely as the center-defender) during defense are the most important ones, and that her playing ability on defense is crucial. There are differences in play depending upon whether the center-defender operates as an individual or if she is working with the team as a whole. Her responsibilities will vary depending on whether she is solely in charge of the hole-man, or if she is getting help from her teammates.

Individual tactics

When the top driver (player #3) is playing defense, she will assume the center-defender position (position #6) since she is the closest point in relation to her goalie. Often there is a direct duel between the center and the center-defender. This is how the center-defender controls the game - when she can successfully stop the center player on her own. When we talk about individual tactics of the center-defender we assume that other players on defense are not involved in helping out with stopping the center and that they are playing a "pressing" - or pressure - defense. Pressure defense means that each player is in constant contact with her counterpart on the opposing team. Pressure defense is played with always placing one arm at the opponent's shoulder, disabling her from getting the ball without being fouled. By being solely in charge of the hole-man, center-defender is not receiving any assistance from her teammates in stopping the action in front of the goal. Figure 5 below shows that the top driver, who is player #3 on offense, becomes player #6, the center-defender, on defense. As I mentioned in the notes on the illustrations, the dark players are playing defense in my figures, and the light are on offense.

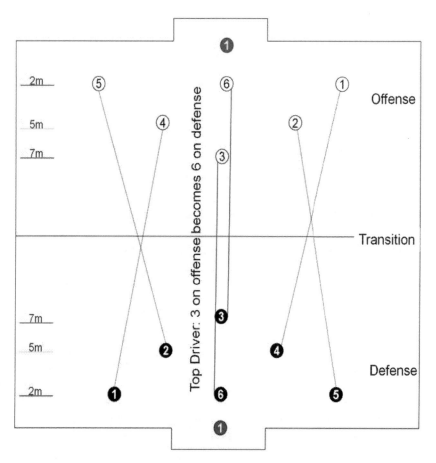

FIGURE 5: Top Driver #3 on Offense Becomes #6 on Defense

Sometimes, a direct duel can imply violence under the water, with as much legal fighting as possible. But there are other ways of playing defense when you are the center-defender guarding the hole-man. You could have a defensive strategy with a considerable amount of contact and less fighting, or you could barely touch the other player and swim around them a great deal.

Each of these tactics has advantages in different situations, and is based on the body morphology of the player on defense versus the player on offense.

When you think of a defensive strategy, you typically think of one with lots of contact and lots of fighting. Usually this is reserved for the center-defenders who possess a lot of strength compared to the center player with whom she is dueling. In the battle itself, the center-defender can easily overcome the player in the center position and therefore can control the game of that player. For the casual observer, the contact appears to be extremely violent, but it's okay - the defender attacks the player with the ball for as long as she can – resorting to dunking if necessary – until the player lets go of the ball. To simplify, that's how you draw a foul.

When you have a center-defender who is not as strong as the center player, it is possible to compensate for this by having them position themselves better in relation to the ball. They are less likely to win a duel, but can prevent the ball from being passed into the hole by always positioning themselves in the passing lanes. By using this strategy and employing a little bit more swimming, your medium-sized center-defender can control the game as effectively as a physically strong center-defender can. There is still contact with the hole-man; after every pass, the center-defender repositions herself in between the ball and the hole-man and then puts her hand on the hole-man's shoulder, keeping the ball in her line of vision at all times.

When you have a lightweight player in the center-defender position, there should be no contact with the hole-man. The reason for this approach is because there is a risk that a lighter center-defender could get pulled by the hole-man, and lose the fronting position that she worked hard for. She is looking back and forth between the ball and the center player, making sure that the center player doesn't move, so the center-defender isn't in the passing lane any more. She is constantly repositioning herself to maintain her position in the passing lanes, but keeping out of the grasp of the hole-man. While this is not legal, for the center player to grab and pull, it is often tolerated. This is an ideal strategy for your fastest swimmer, as a stronger hole-man gets frustrated with all of this swimming around, and often commits an offensive foul.

When you think of your best center-defender/top driver and how she fits into one of the strategies above, you should also be thinking about what kind of person she is. It's important that she have a very strong work ethic and enjoy the physicality of the job she is given. As I mentioned before, I often choose this position as the captain of the team, because of the leadership skills that a person like this possesses. Imagine a German Shepherd – strong, hard working, loyal, vigilant, courageous, tireless, but also easy to control and train. While the German Shepherd doesn't have the best sense of smell, is not the fastest dog, doesn't have the hardest bite, but when you combine all of these traits together, the German Shepherd is the best value for your dollar – an all-around all star.

The center-defender doesn't always have to do everything by herself. She is the leader of the team, and as such she can get help from her teammates to perform up to task. Help can come from the slough from one player, or the slough from multiple players. This happens when the defense plays zone defense, and not pressure defense. Zone defense is usually implemented when there is a strong center player that the center-defender cannot adequately control, or has already made our center-defender get kicked out couple of times.

When help is solicited for the center-defender, it is her job to push the center player towards the side from which help is coming. This push can be aimed at one or more players who are sloughing, and provides an opportunity to prevent the center player from getting the ball.

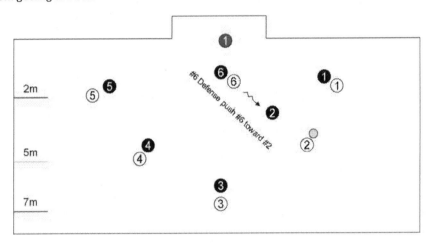

FIGURE 6 : Hole-Defender #6 is Pushing the Hole-Man Toward the Slough

There is a limited opportunity for the goalie to help the center-defender as well, but this is only employed if the rest of the team plays tight defense. If the goalie swims out to steal the ball, the center-defender has to raise both arms up and show the referee that she is not dunking the center player. Most often, when the center-defender is not directly behind the center player, but on either side of her, the goalie can swim to the opposite side and steal the ball, as shown in Figure 7 below. The goalie has to be careful, because there could be a surprise shot at the cage instead of a pass to the hole-man, while the goalie is busy swimming out. After every foul, the goalie can only swim out if the player with the ball is inside the 5 meter line. When a foul is committed outside of the 5 meter line, that player can shoot at the goal instead of passing to the center, which would be a surprise to the goalie, who had been expecting that she would pass the ball into the hole and not shoot.

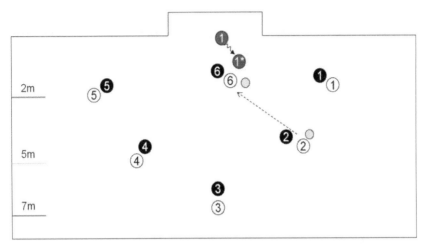

FIGURE 7: Goalie Goes Out to Steal the Ball from the Center Player

DEFENSIVE TACTICS OF THE CENTER-DEFENDER USING THE TEAM AS A WHOLE

These tactics use the collective expertise of the team and have the team function as one unit. The center-defender is like the conductor of an orchestra – calling on her teammates to perform at the right moment. When defense comes from the center-defender in conjunction with the defense of the whole team, there are several scenarios where this can be used; when your team is defending from counterattack, or defending with an equal number of players, or when you are in a man-down situation.

TACTICS OF THE CENTER-DEFENDER DEFENDING FROM COUNTERATTACK

Clearly, your team needs to have a method to stop any counterattack, and the best way to create this method is with rules that everybody knows and follows. One of the first rules is that you must slow down or – even better - prevent that first pass from the goalie. You do that by playing pressure defense everywhere across the pool after your team has lost the ball. This strategy is fairly easy to understand and implement – and works pretty well to slow down play. I should add that when the first pass is finally made from the goalie, your players should remain pressing on their assigned players and then making ordinary fouls as soon as their player gets the ball.

It's crucial that everybody on the team cooperates and knows exactly what to do at every single moment during transition.

The second tactic requires a little more practice to make it perfect. It still requires that your team pressures the first pass from the goalie, but the team goes back on defense in a regimented fashion. In Serbian we call it "The Funnel." In this strategy, the top driver (player #3) sprints back to her defensive position in front of her goalie, looking to make a foul or pick up any escaping player. While she is moving straight from her position on offense to her position on defense, players #2 & 4, swim so that they create a "bottleneck" or funnel, to force the opposing players to swim in outside water on their way to their offensive positions.

By creating this bottleneck these players will be able to stop/take over any player who is cutting through the middle. The player who is most often late to come back on defense, and whose player needs to get picked up, is player #6, or the hole-man. This is because her role during the offense is very physically taxing and she is usually the slowest swimmer on the team because of her wide frame.

Just as players #2 & 4 were creating a bottleneck, players #1 & 5 are making sure that they conquer inside water as well – their defenders are typically on the inside position when the ball is lost, and so players #1 & 5 need to sprint inwards until they have forced their counterparts to the outside water. The figure below indicates the movement of each player from offense (white) to defense (black). All players on defense should look to make a foul when the players they are guarding are in possession of the ball, in order to slow down the counterattack and buy time, so that the counterattack doesn't result in a man-up situation.

This transitional defense is also known as immediate defense and as you've seen everyone has a role to play in it, ensuring the counterattack is slowed down and the foul is committed. Immediate defense ends when the player whose opponent escaped catches up with her player, and the defense is set up 6 on 6 in the other end of the pool.

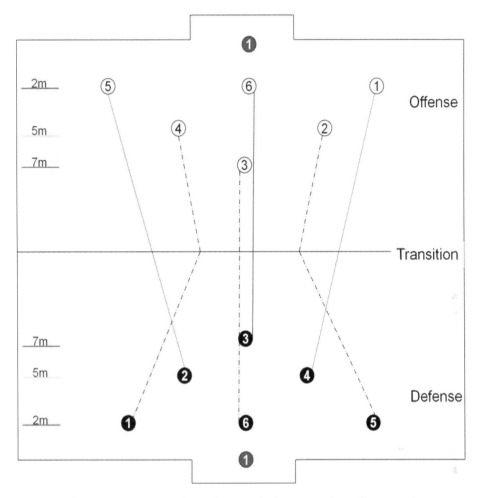

FIGURE 8: Defending from Counterattack: Specific Positioning in Transition from Offense To Defense

TACTICS OF DEFENDING WITH THE SAME NUMBER OF PLAYERS (6 ON 6)

For this situation, we can defend with pressure defense or we can defend with zone defense. When using pressure defense, we are assuming that the center-defender can take care of the center player by herself; either fronting, siding, or playing from behind. As I mentioned before, the most desirable pressure defense from a center-defender is being in the passing lanes, which means being in between the ball and the center player at all times.

Usually when the ball is in possession of players #4 or 5 (on the left side of the field), the center-defender is on the left side as well. When the ball is in the possession of player #3, the center-defender is in front of the hole-man. Finally, when the ball is in the possession of players # 1 or 2 (on the right side of the field), center-defender is also on the right side of the field. The point is to get in the passing lanes, fronting the hole-man and being in between the player with the ball and the center player.

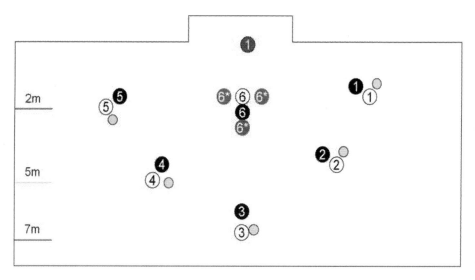

FIGURE 9: Position of the Center-Defender Depending Where the Ball is During Pressure Defense

Unlike the positioning of the center-defender (player #6) in a pressure defense, during zone defense, the center-defender is always positioned *behind* the center player – she does not front or side the hole-man. Her job is to block the shots, holding one arm up and the other arm on the shoulder of the center player so she can get up higher. Usually the reason for the team playing zone defense is because our center-defender cannot control the hole-man by herself. The hole-defender must push the hole-man as far from the goal as possible, allowing the possibilities of other players sloughing and stealing the ball in case it is passed to the hole-man. In Figure 10 below, I have shown the positioning of the center-defender when there is sloughing coming from player #3. It is worth mentioning that the slough can come from a group of players as well and then pushing will be directed toward those players.

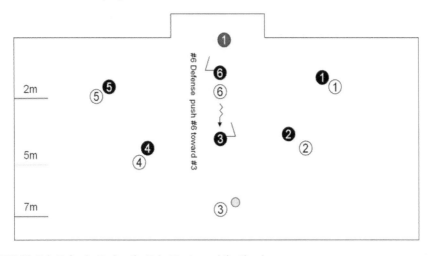

FIGURE 10: Hole-Defender Pushes the Hole-Man toward the Slough

TACTICS OF THE CENTER-DEFENDER DURING MAN-DOWN POWER PLAY

Even though the center-defender is the player who most often gets kicked out, her role (or anyone else's who assumes her position after the kick out) is the most important on the man-down power play. This is because she can get up high, blocking the shots, and she is fast to move from one player to the other, sliding while treading and blocking the shots. When the kick-out happens, somebody needs to crash toward the cage, guarding the hole-man (because the center-defender most likely got kicked out) and protecting the goal and the space around player #6. If the hole-man defender gets kicked out, defensive players #2, 3 & 4 will all crash toward the hole-man and usually player #3 on defense (top driver's defender) is the one who "sticks" with the hole-man and becomes player #5 in Figure 11 below. By having the closest player crash toward the hole-man, we will ensure

29

that the center player isn't alone in front of the goal for long. I address this scenario in more depth – called immediate defense – in the Man Down chapter.

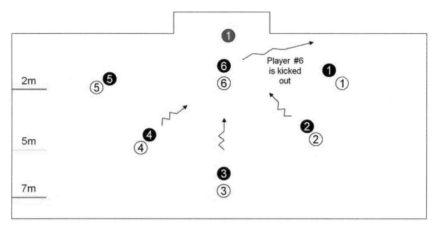

FIGURE 11: Center-Defender Positioning During Immediate Defense

Now that we have the "new" center-defender in position #5, she is situated in between the posts in the 4:2 system of play as pictured below in Figure 12, and her assignments are:

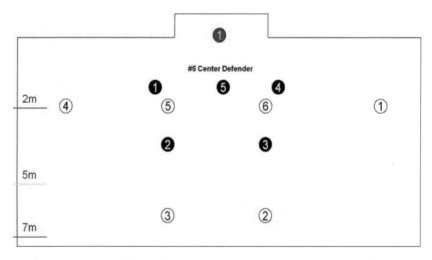

FIGURE 12: Center-Defender Positioning After Immediate Defense

To block diagonal/cross-cage shots from outside players, and to cover the players # 5 & 6 on offense - that are positioned on the posts. As it is shown in Figure 13 below, when player #3 on offense has the ball, the center-defender, now playing in position #5, should get close to player #5 on offense and prevent the ball from getting passed to player #5. She should raise her left arm, blocking diagonal shots. When player #2 on offense has the ball, top driver (player #5) should slide toward player #6 on offense, and prevent the ball getting to player #6 on offense. Her other job is to again raise her right arm blocking diagonal shots.

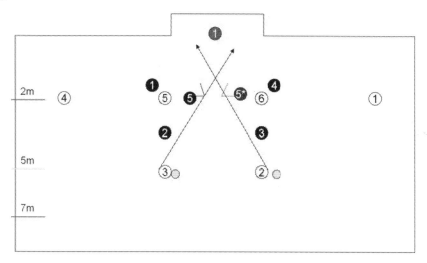

FIGURE 13: Center-Defender Tactics When the Players #2 & 3 Have the Ball

To ensure that the two players on the posts (offensive players #5 & 6) don't get the ball from wing players #1 & 4. When the wing players have the ball, her job is to block any cross-cage shots as is shown in Figure 14 below, and to place the other arm on the post player's shoulders. As the ball is passed around, she slides back and forth between players #5 & 6, staying in between these two players at all times.

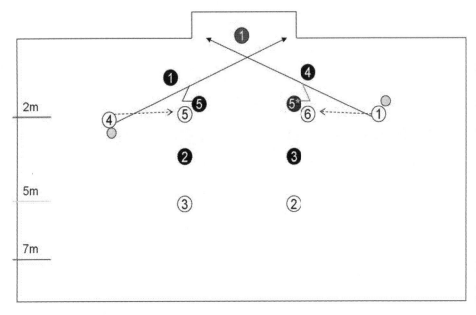

FIGURE 14: Guarding Players 5 & 6 and Blocking Cross-Cage Shots

To ensure the wing players cannot score in the closer part of the cage. When the center-defender moves to one of the wing positions her assignments are to block shots by raising her right arm when player #4 has the ball, or her left arm when player #1 has the ball (see Figure 15 below).

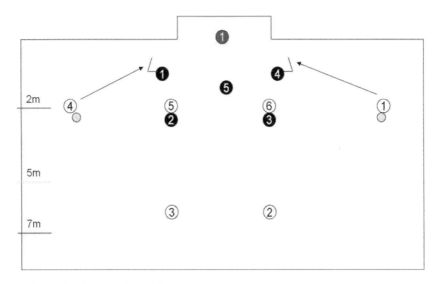

FIGURE 15: Blocking the Closer-Cage Shots

<u>To press the players on the posts</u>. Another responsibility when the center-defender is in the wing position is to press the players on the posts when the ball is in the hands of players #2 or 3. She is also blocking any shots coming from those positions by raising her arm up.

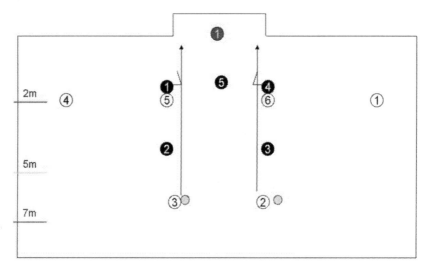

FIGURE 16: Guarding Players on the Posts and Blocking Shots from Outside

The defensive play leans heavily on the center-defender position; that is player #6 when we have an even number of players, player #5 when we are man-down, or any other position that she finds herself in, as I have described in the text above. The way that the game is refereed determines many tactics that the center-defender uses and so she must remain aware and flexible during the entire defensive game. She will always start the game with full aggressiveness, but she may need to back off if she gets kicked out often.

I hope I have demonstrated to the reader how important the center-defender's role is. She is the most flexible, all around player on the team, and as we move to discussing the offensive play tactics, you will have an even better view of this position.

Top Driver Tactics During Offense – Position #3

Now that we have covered defensive tactics for the center-defender and the team as a whole, we switch over to the offensive part of the game, and the terminology changes to Top Driver and we focus on position #3 in my figures. This player is at the furthest point from the opponent's cage – the top of the action – so she has an excellent view of the front court offense and must possess a strong shot in order to score from that far away. While her defensive tactics must be strong and her ability to block shots and shut down the hole-man is crucial, it is also imperative that she can pass the ball accurately to an open player and can score on offense. When she comes back from defense, where she played center-defender (black player #6), she will assume position #3 on offense (white).

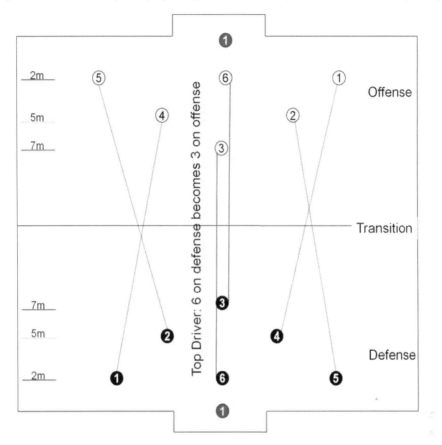

FIGURE 17: Player #6 on Defense Becomes #3 on Offense

Again, I will break down the differences in play depending upon whether the top driver operates as an individual or if she is working with the team as a whole.

INDIVIDUAL TACTICS OF THE TOP DRIVER

When we think of the offensive tactics of the top driver as an individual player, we are looking at what she can do on offense individually. The play is different depending on which defensive strategies the opposing team employs. She can be guarded with pressure defense, slough against her, or slough against some other player.

35

In the play against pressure defense, the main goal of the top driver is to get open from her defender. She will accomplish this by swiftly moving in different directions and precisely judging when to go for these openings. When she moves towards an empty space in the front court, she will draw her defender to her, which can open another one of her teammates up, or create an opportunity for herself to get a pass which can lead to a shot - hopefully a score.

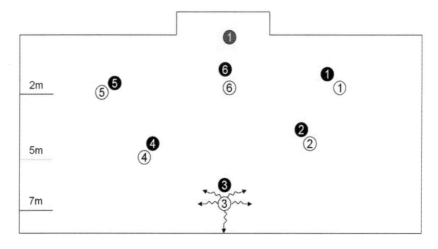

FIGURE 18: Top Driver Tactics against Pressure Defense

During the slough against the top driver, she can get the ball, but she is too far away to shoot. She needs to worm in forward while faking the goalie, and as she gets closer a few different things can happen. She can either pass the ball to an open teammate, shoot if the shot is open, or she can pass to one side and drive in to the opposite side of the cage, trying to free up the middle so that the ball can go into the hole.

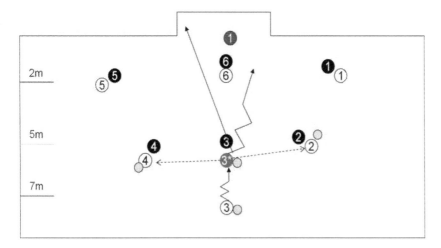

FIGURE 19: Slough Against Top Driver and Suggested Tactics to Break the Slough

When the slough is aimed at another player on the team, the top driver is pressed, but another player on the team is open. The player who is open can get the ball and as in the example above, can worm in closer to the cage so that she can take a higher percentage shot. Alternately, she can drive, trying to pick up her defender, freeing up the hole so that the ball can be passed to the center player. If she decides to drive, other players need to slide out, filling up the gap she left. In my figure below, the players who need to slide out are players #3, 2, & 1. One thing that you need to keep in mind is that player #4 in this situation shouldn't start her drive as the shot clock is ending, instead the drive should happen in the first 20 seconds of the offense. During the last 5-10 seconds of offense she should be starting to go back on defense so that she can get there on time and not get burned. Because the slough is not directed towards the top driver, but at another player, the top driver's job is to let player #4 take the lead I suggested. As the shot clock is running out, whether the shot was taken or not, the top driver can backstroke out, keeping an eye on the play as she readies herself for defense.

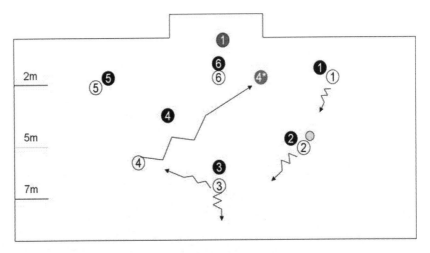

FIGURE 20: Slough against Player #4 and Suggested Tactics to Break the Slough

GROUP TACTICS OF THE TOP DRIVER DURING OFFENSE

Now I will describe the tactics of the top driver when she is working with one of her teammates. This cooperation will result in either the top driver or the partner she is playing with getting open. These tactics are most applicable when the defense is playing pressure defense, though some of these tactics can be utilized against zone defense as well.

The top driver can set the pick on any of her teammates, though it makes most sense to set the pick on players #2 or 4, because they are closest to her and because she is not going to clog up the middle as much as she would if she were to set the pick on players #1, 5 or 6. Player #3 swims toward the defending player #2 who she blocks, putting herself behind defensive player #2. In that moment, offensive player #2 swims around the pick and goes to the opposite post. After offensive player #2 swam around the pick, the top driver should crash in the same manner towards the other post, looking to get open. Now we have either player #2 or player #3 getting open for a pass from player #4 and we have successfully broken the pressure defense.

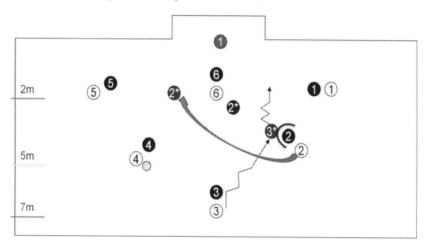

FIGURE 21: Setting a Pick

The top driver can drive towards the left post, and as soon as she swims past player #4, that triggers player #4 to swim over player #3's legs, heading for the opposite post. As in most offensive tactics, the goal of this play is to get open from the defender with help from one of the teammates from either side. As a result of a crossover done by players #3 & 4, their appropriate defenders won't be able to guard them because of the entanglement they caused. This drill is designed to get one of the defenders kicked out, so the players doing the crossover have to have that in mind and instigate the kick out as much as possible. Aside from the top driver crossing over with player #4 or 2, the crossover is possible with players #2 & 4 as well.

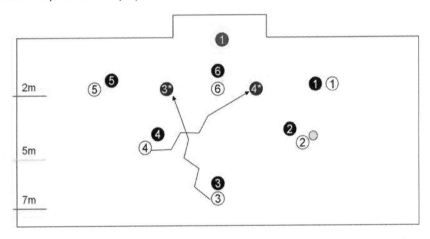

FIGURE 22: Crossover Involving Top Driver and Left Driver

The hole-man can set a pick on one of the driver's defenders. Collaboration of the center player with one of the teammates from the outside positions refers to setting a pick on any player that needs to get open. The pick-setting can be initiated from the hole-man (when she swims out towards the outside defender and blocks defender #4), or can be initiated by the outside player (when one of the players #2, 3, or 4 drives towards the post and center player #6 slides out and blocks her defender). The difference is who starts swimming first; the hole-man in one situation or the driver. I'll show the first example in the figure below.

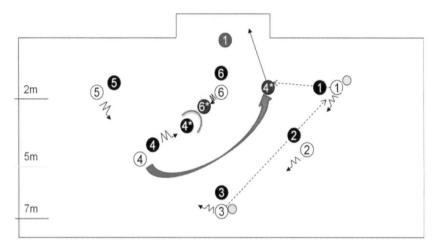

FIGURE 23: Center Blocks the Driver's Defender (Player #6 Blocks Player #4's Defender)

The next section deals with the tactics of the top driver when she is working with the whole team. The end result of this teamwork will be that someone on the team – often, but not necessarily, the top driver – will get open and have an opportunity to score.

Top driver tactics during counterattack. During counterattack, the top driver has a prominent role because very often she is the one who will have the advantage over her defender. Let's not forget that she was center-defender during defense and now - after the ball was stolen - she became top driver, pushing against the hole-man on the transition. The reason why I expect to see the top driver beat her defender on the transition is because she just spent about 20 seconds on the hole-man's back during the defense, "hanging on her" from behind, and therefore should have more energy to sprint across the pool than the hole-man would. This defensive wrestling and offensive sprinting repeated throughout the whole game can only be done if the player possesses the physical stamina and force of will required to get the job done. This is to say that not everybody can play in the top driver position. The figure below shows the top driver swimming from defense (black position #6) to offense (white position #3).

On transition, the team as a whole, going through counterattack, has to move in the way that the drawing shows below. That means that the players will change their positions, just like center-defender becomes top driver, right driver becomes right wing (black position #4 becomes white position #1) etc. After you have studied the way each player is supposed to move on this transition, the next thing I suggest on a counterattack is that the ball is passed from the goalie (after she blocked the shot) to player #4 who becomes player #1 on offense. Somewhere around midcourt, player #1 must turn and do the backstroke (still continuously swimming) and receive a wet pass in front of her from the goalie. Then she will swim with the ball to the 2 meter line, where she will stop, fake the goalie, and pass to player #3, the top driver, who will take a shot. If the top driver is left-handed, this action can go on the other side as well. I also want to add that this is not the only way to do a counterattack, but it is the basic building block that your team must master before working on the variations. Everything in this counterattack action is predicated on the assumption that the top driver will sprint back faster than her defender and can remain open to take a shot. If somebody else is open, then by all means they should be given the ball and allowed to take a shot.

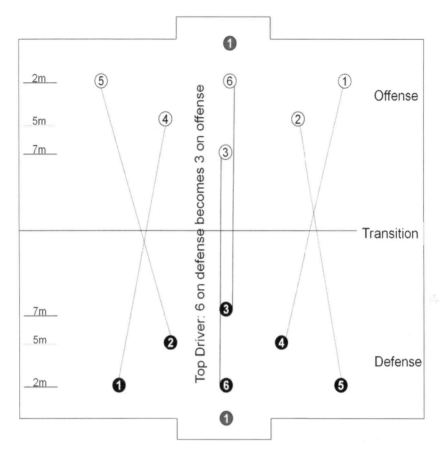

FIGURE 24: Player #6 on Defense Becomes #3 on Offense

Top driver tactics with an even number of players. Because of her central position, it's obvious that the top driver is a playmaker and is the organizer of the action during 6 on 6 situation. She can see the whole pool at the same time, and is a strong player with an excellent shot. At any time, she can pass the ball to either side of the offense, or to the hole-man. During 6 on 6 situation, her teammates should help her get open and take the shot as often as possible. In the examples above, I have detailed the ways that the top driver can get open in both a pressure and a zone defense situation. The figure below shows the top driver's central role on the team.

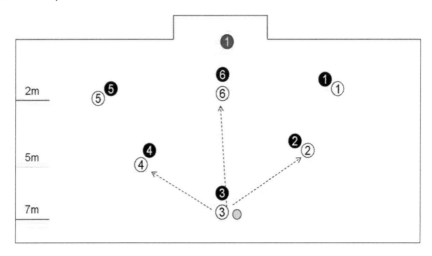

FIGURE 25: Top Driver Playmaking during 6:6 Offense

Top driver tactics during man-up situations. As we mentioned before, the top driver has to have a strong shot and strong legs. Because of these two strengths, there are two options for positioning during man-up in the 4:2 system – the first is to play in position # 3, where she can use her strong shot and the second is to play in position #5, where she must use her strong legs. One post is reserved for the top driver, and the other post should be reserved for the player who played the hole-man. In the 3:3 system, she is most useful in position #3. Less often on the man-up situations, top driver can play on the right wing (position #1) when she is left-handed.

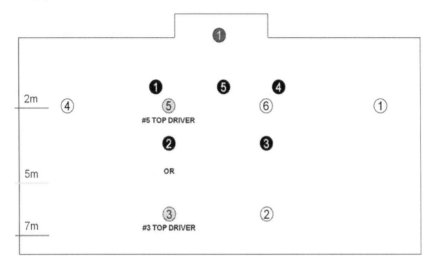

FIGURE 26: Top Driver Positioning In a 4:2 Man-Up Situation

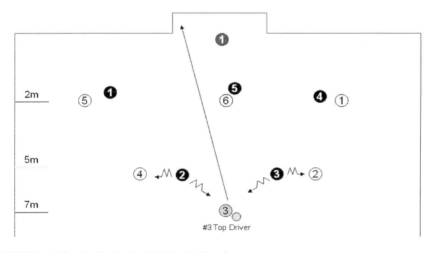

FIGURE 27: Top Driver Positioning In a 3:3 Man-Up Situation

45

In this day and age, the play of the center-defender is very complex but mastery of it is crucial for achieving optimal results. From what I presented in the text, you can see that there are many ways to play in this position, and a lot of it depends on the qualities and characteristics of the player.

TACTICS DURING THE MAN-DOWN SITUATION

Now we are moving slightly away from focusing on the top driver, and discussing each player on the team.

There is nothing in water polo that presents such a regular opportunity – or handicap – as the Man-up/Man-down situation. When a player gets kicked out, it's a huge advantage for the team who now has a man-up situation. And it happens all the time – depending on what kind of defense is played. During zone defense, man-down is minimal, but during pressure defense, it can happen sometimes 10 to 20 times per game! If you do the math and are 50% successful in stopping a goal during a man-down situation, you can prevent 5 to 10 goals. That is why skilled coaches take ample time to practice this aspect. And again – defense is key. Truly excellent teams have a high success rate in stopping the opposing team from scoring during man-up. That's why I want to devote a significant amount of time to discussing the man-down situation.

In man-down situations, the **Top Driver** becomes the **Center-defender** or **Hole-defender**, as I've already explained. She can assume any position, but most often – and most preferably – she is in position #5. In the two illustrations below, there is a 3:3 system and a 4:2 system for offense, and it shows where the center-defender is typically located.

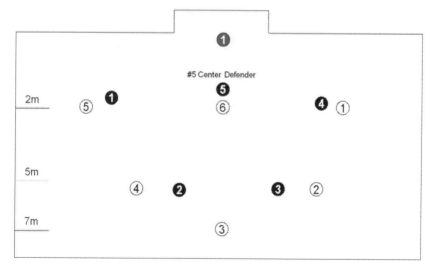

FIGURE 28: Top Driver Positioning During Man-Down in System 3:3

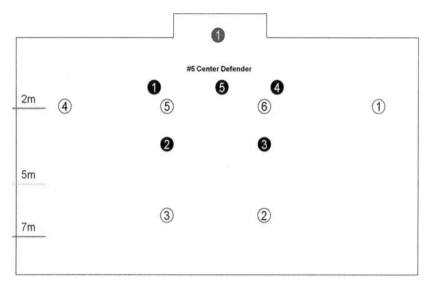

FIGURE 29: Top Driver Positioning During Man-Down in System 4:2

THE SYSTEMS OF PLAYING IN A MAN-DOWN SITUATION

Protecting the space in front of the cage so that the opponent is unable to score is crucial during man-down. I look at the man-down as a type of zone defense where the players involved are in charge of protecting the space in front of the goal as much as the space inside of the cage. The secondary goal of the man-down defense is to make it easy for the player who is in the least preferred position for taking the shot, to take the shot. A lot of time needs to be spent on practicing all of the possibilities of what the other team might do during their man-up situation, so when the time comes, your team's man-down tactics are ready as an answer to all man-up options the other team might have. All players have to keep their cool and remain focused, because if one mistake is made, the team that's on the man-up can turn it into a score. Man-down requires a lot of jumps, swimming, sliding, and treading which are the reasons why the team needs to be very well conditioned in order to have the energy to do it with full power.

The play during the defense of man-down also depends on the positioning of the opposing team. The drawings below will explain the movements of the players through all the major systems of defense on man-down situations. Breaking these concepts down into examples will take the reader to the next level of understanding, and will shed light on the way that I, as coach, see the game.

Immediate Defense on Man-Down

Before we go into the different systems of defense during man-down, it's worth mentioning that one thing that the defensive team needs to do in order to protect itself is to be skilled at immediate defense. It is very common that after a player has been kicked out (most often the center-defender #6), the hole-man (now without the defender) can pass the ball to any outside player, who then passes the ball back to her, and she then takes the shot. As a consequence of this double pass the coaches have developed the immediate defense.

Immediate defense is described by having outside defenders – players #2, 3 or 4 swim to guard the hole-man immediately after their teammate (defensive player #6) has been kicked out, so that the center player #6 on offense doesn't get an easy pass and a shot on the goal. Another reason for crashing into the hole is to get into defensive positions faster in order to better protect your team against the man-up. The crash itself needs to be done immediately while the whistle is being blown signaling the kick out. I suggest that all outside players (#2, 3 & 4) crash towards the center player in order to avoid confusion on the team expecting that someone else will take responsibility. Of course only one defensive player will stay on player #6 on offense (usually player #3), and other two will go to their positions depending upon what system offense sets up, and depending on what the tactic is that the defensive team will play. After we made sure that player #6 on offense is being guarded, the defense can transition from immediate defense to one of the man-down defensive tactics I described above. Being successful at the immediate defense is an important part of the game, since inability to do so can result in the loss of the morale of the team and is especially hard on the goalie who loses confidence if the opposing team gets an easy shot on him.

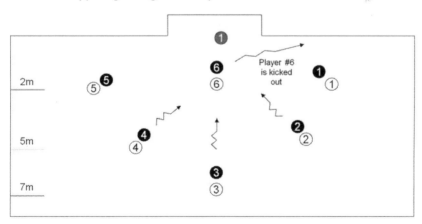

FIGURE 30: Immediate Defense with Players #2, 3 & 4 Crashing Into the Hole

DEFENSE 3:2 FOR OFFENSE 3:3

There are a few different possibilities to defend when you play man down defense against system 3:3. In the first scenario, our players on defense should set up in system 3:2. This means that all players at the 2 meter line are covered man-to-man, and the 5 meter line is dynamically covered in a zone defense. Players #2 & 3 on defense are jumping in between 3 players on offense, attacking and retreating looking to make a steal, make a foul or just have the shot clock run out.

When player #3 has the ball, it's necessary that players #2 & 3 jump at her pretending they are going for a foul. This is done by doing a technique of "rear back", or RB (a couple of strokes forward/freestyle and couple of strokes backwards/backstroke). If the player doesn't pass the ball in time, players #2 & 3 on defense absolutely have to go for a foul or even better a steal. During all this time player #5 on defense has to have her arm up and protect from the cross-cage corner shots that will come from players #2, 3 & 4. Also during the entire action the wing players have to strictly press players #1 & 5, and after the shot, they should go for the rebound.

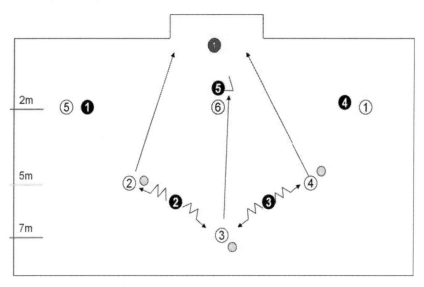

FIGURE 31: Defense 3:2 for Offense 3:3 – Scenario #1

A similar situation happens in the second scenario. Players are positioned the same way with some subtle differences. Center-defender (player #5) again defends cross-cage with her arm up, and defensive wings #1 & 4 will slide into the shooting lanes, blocking the shots coming from players #2, 3 & 4. As in the previous example, players #2 & 3 jump at the top three players, #2, 3 & 4, pretending to go for a foul by employing the RB technique.

When player #2 is taking a shot, defensive player #1 will slide to the left, getting into the shooting lane, holding her left arm up. During that same time, defensive player #4 is pressing player #1 on offense, waiting to pick up the rebound. When player #3 is taking a shot, defensive players #1 & 4 will slide to the left or right, respectively, holding their left or right arms up to block the shot. When player #4 is taking a shot, defensive player #4 will slide to the right, holding her right arm up, blocking the shot, while defensive player #1 presses her opponent – player #5 – going for the rebound after the shot.

This tactic enables the defense to swiftly go to counterattack with players #2 & 3 that were on defense, sprinting now to offense against player #3 who was on offense. This gives a two-on-one advantage when they go on counterattack. The key to successful defense is that players #2 & 3 don't overly commit to one of the outside players #2, 3 & 4, and inadvertently leave the other side open. For example, if they focus too much on player #4, they will leave player #2 open. It's worth noting that usually player #3 on offense will prepare the shot for players #2 & 4 and not take the shot herself, so defense shouldn't chase player #3 too much.

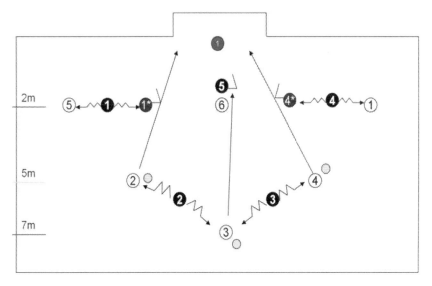

FIGURE 32: Defense 3:2 for Offense 3:3 – Scenario #2

Umbrella Defense for 3:3 Offense

A third scenario when the offense is set up 3:3 is to set up an "Umbrella" defense. For this tactic, the defenders position themselves in between the players on offense, dynamically covering the outside players. The center-defender #5, who is positioned behind the hole-man as is shown in the figure, is guarding her statically, raising the arm up and blocking shots from the outside. As soon as any of the outside players get the ball, the closest defense player (sometimes both of them) has to sprint towards that player and attack with the RB or commit a regular foul. There are several benefits to this system; when the defense positions itself like this, the offense doesn't have much time to get in good position in order to take a good shot at the goal because the defense is very close to each of them. Also, the offense will not expect this kind of defense so it can be a good element of surprise when it is not done often and if it's combined with a regular defense (previous example), system 3:2.

When the ball is stolen or a shot missed this is a great chance to go to a counterattack; either two-on-one or four-on-three. One flaw of this defense is that it's physically challenging for the defense, therefore the players need to be in great shape.

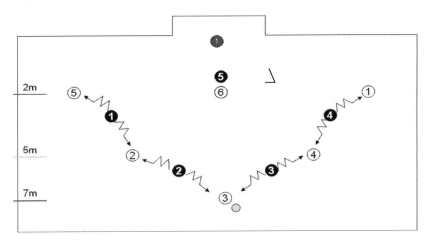

FIGURE 33: Umbrella Defense for 3:3 Offense

Defense 3:2 for offense 4:2

In this section, I describe the positioning and which arm is up for each of the 5 players who are in possession of the ball during the man-down situation when the offense is set up in the 4:2 configuration.

One of the ways of defending in this scenario is to place three defenders on the first line (2 meter) and two defenders on the second line 5-6 meter (aligned with the posts). This kind of defense is usually present in the beginning of the man-up situation before the offense starts shifting/sliding in order to open up one of the players. It's very important to add that each player on defense is responsible for two players on offense and blocking appropriate space in the goal.

In the next section, we will look at each defensive player's duties and responsibilities in terms of what two players on offense each one is guarding, and what part of the cage is being blocked.

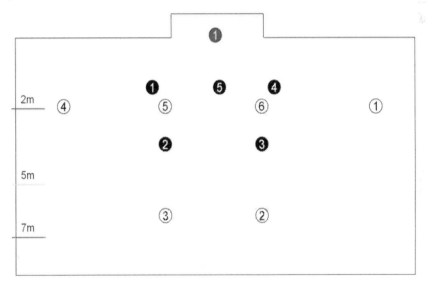

FIGURE 34: Defense 3:2 for Offense 4:2

Player #1 on defense has the assignment to defend the closer-cage from the shots that come from players #3, 4 or 5. When the ball is not in the hands of player #4 on offense, player #1 on defense has to take care of player #5, getting behind her and putting one hand on her shoulder and with the other hand blocking the shots that might be coming from outside. Under no circumstance can player #5 get the ball for the quick shot. In the figure below we see how player #1 on defense moves depending on where the ball is.

When player #3 on offense has the ball, our player #1 has to again protect the closer-cage raising her arm up. If the ball flies from player #3 to player #5 our player has to protect the closer-cage and attack player #5 and prevent her from taking the shot - going for the ball not the body of the player.

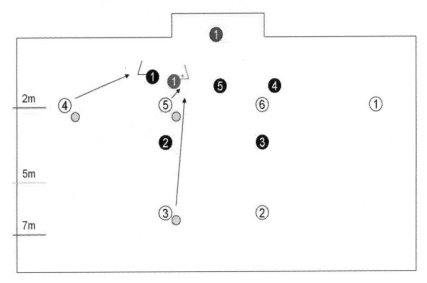

FIGURE 35: Player #1 Blocks Closer-Cage Shots from Players #3, 4 or 5

When player #2 has the ball, our player has to press player #5 and with her arm up defend the cross-cage (it's still the same part of the goal, but since player #2 has the ball, it's a cross-cage shot for her). In the case of a lob shot from player #2, it's our player again who has to make that save.

When player #1 has the ball, our player has to stay on player #5, with her left arm up blocking the cross-cage shot as well as a lob shot.

When player #6 has the ball, the only assignment of our player is to strictly press player # 5 and lift her left arm up, blocking the cross-cage.

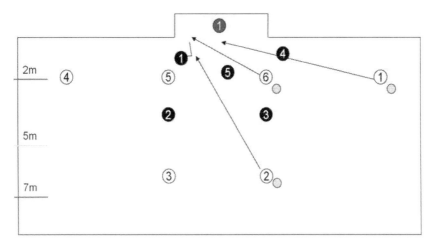

FIGURE 36: Player #1 Blocks Cross-Cage Shots from Players #1, 2 or 6

MOVEMENT AND RESPONSIBILITIES FOR DEFENDER #2

For this position it is very important to have an agile player that is fast to react/jump/tread. Her job is to block shots from the outside and to guard/press player #5 on the post.

When player #4 has the ball, our player (#2) has to press player #5 on offense and to put her body in the passing lane in between players #4 & 2 on offense so that she can steal that pass that goes from player #4 to player #2. If player #2 on offense slides to the left, our player has to get into the shooting lane and block the cross-cage shot with her left arm.

When player #3 has the ball, our player #2 has to be in front of player #5 on offense and if player #3 fakes/pumps the goalie for too long and/or comes too close to the goal, she has to attack her. Her arm has to be constantly up defending the closer-corner.

When player #1 has the ball, our player has to adapt her movement based on the movements of player #5 who is on offense. That means if player #5 gets outside of the 2 meter line it is her job to follow her. Player #2 is responsible for blocking the shot from player #3 if a pass was made from player #1 to player #3.

55

When player #6 has the ball, her job is to guard player #5 especially if player #5 is outside of the 2 meter line.

If the ball ends up in player #5's hand, our player needs to intervene as soon as possible, especially if player #5 is outside of the 2 meter line.

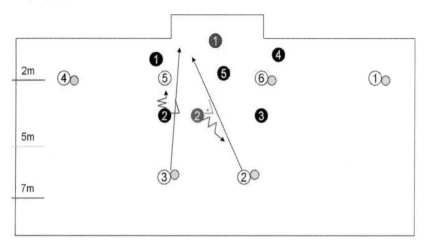

FIGURE 37: Player #2 Controls Player #5 and Blocks the Shots from Players #2 & 3

MOVEMENT AND RESPONSIBILITIES FOR POSITION #3

Just like defensive position #2, the player in defensive position #3 should be an agile player, able to jump from player to player based on where the ball is. Her main role is to guard player #6 and to block the shots from players #2 & 3.

When player #1 has the ball, player #3 has to come back on the first line of defense (2 meters) and press player #6 and at the same time get her body in the passing lane so that she can steal the pass that goes from player #1 to player #3. If player #6 is sliding out to get more open, our player shuts her down by either blocking or stealing the pass or by positioning herself so that the ball is not passed to her.

When player #2 has the ball, our player has to push against player #6 where she was positioned previously and lift her arm up in order to block the closer-corner. If player #2 comes too close to the goal and/or is faking the goalie for too long (more than 3 fakes) player #3 has to attack her by either forcing her to pass somewhere else or to make the foul on player #2.

In the worst case scenario, if player #6 gets the ball, player #3 has to react as quickly as possible and stop that shot by going for the ball not the body of player #6.

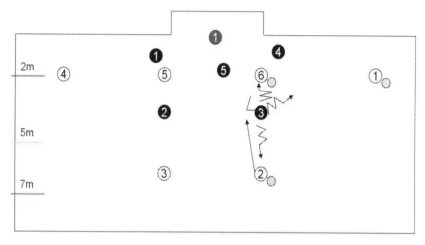

FIGURE 38: Player #3 Controls Player #6 and Blocks the Shots from Player #2

When player #3 has the ball, our player has to make sure that she protects against a cross-cage shot. If player #3 on offense is sliding to the right, our player attacks her with her arm up defending the cross-cage shot.

When player #4 has the ball, our player has to take care of player #6 and follow her movements. If player #6 slides out to the 3-4 meter line it's our player's responsibility to follow her and not let her get that pass. Also if the ball is passed from player #4 to player #2, she has to block that shot by quickly switching from guarding player #6 to being in the shooting lane of player #2.

When player #5 has the ball, our player has to strictly guard player #6 and prevent any possible pass that could come from player #5 to player #6.

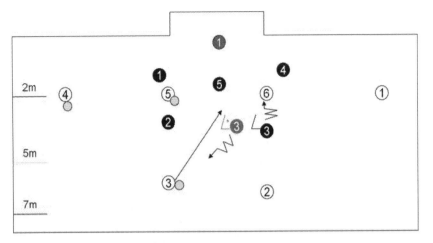

FIGURE 39: Player #3 Slides to the Side, Blocking Shots from Player #3

MOVEMENT AND RESPONSIBILITIES FOR POSITION #4

Player #4 has the same assignments as player #1, but is simply on the opposite side of the goal. When player #1 has the ball our player has to protect the closer-corner with the left arm up (whether or not player #1 is left-handed or right-handed).

When player #2 has the ball our player is responsible for covering player #6 (placing one arm on her shoulder) and protecting the closer-cage corner from a shot (by raising the other arm up). When player #6 is on the 2 meter line it's our player's responsibility to prevent her from getting that pass. When player #6 is sliding outside of the 2 meter line, she becomes the responsibility of defensive player #3.

When player #3 on offense has the ball, our player has to stay on player #6 and to protect the cross-cage shots by raising one arm up and placing the other hand on the shoulder of player #6.

When player #4 has the ball, our player has to stay on player #6 and if there is a lob shot, she blocks that shot and picks up the rebound.

When player #5 has the ball, our player has to stay on player #6 with the arm up defend the cross-cage.

In the worst case scenario, when player #6 has the ball, our player has to defend the closer-cage with the arm up and go for the ball trying to knock it out of player's #6 hand.

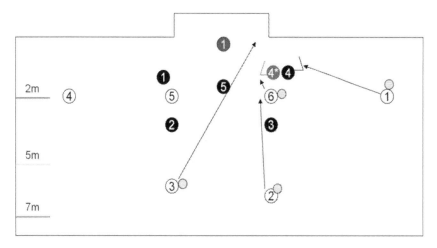

FIGURE 40: Player #4 Controls Player #6 and Blocks the Shots from Player #1, And 2

MOVEMENT AND RESPONSIBILITIES FOR POSITION #5

Player #5 on defense is the Center-defender and therefore the most important player on defending man-down situations. She has to be the most responsible player on the team as well as tread water the best and get high out of the water to block the shots.

When player #1 has the ball our player #5 has to cover player #6 first and then to make sure that the closer-cage corner is protected by lifting her left arm up. At the same time she has to be aware of a possible pass that might go from player #1 to player #6 and be able to prevent this from happening. That is why she will put her right hand on the shoulder of player #6.

When player #2 has the ball, our player has to cover the cross-cage shots (by lifting her right arm up) and this time has to be aware of a possible pass from player #2 to player #5 and prevent this from happening by being close to player #5 and ready to jump on her.

When player #3 has the ball, our player has to protect the cross-cage shots by lifting her left arm, and prevent the ball from going to player #6 by being close to her and ready to react with a strong scissors kick in case that pass happens.

When player #4 has the ball, our players' assignment is to make sure that player #5 doesn't get the ball and to protect the closer-cage corner (by lifting her right arm up). Being in this position our player is able to steal passes that go from player #4 to player #6 and from player #4 to player #1. In the worst case scenario, if the ball does get to player #6 or player #5, our player then needs to protect the cross-cage shots by raising her arm up and not go for a steal or a foul since it would result in another kick out for her team.

In order to be a successful hole-defender in position #5, a player needs to have a great feel for the game and to have strong legs so that she can slide and jump from position to position depending on where the ball is. It's important to add that this is the only position on defense during man-down that has the role of blocking the shots coming from every player on offense, which makes it the most physically demanding.

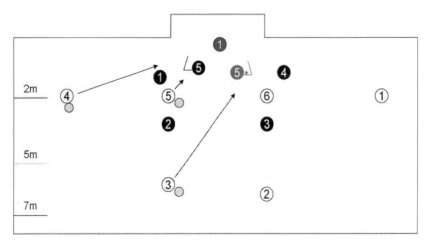

FIGURE 41: Player #5 Blocks the Shots from Players #3, 4 and 5

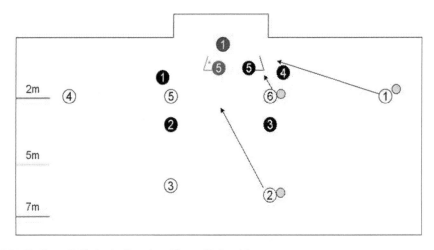

FIGURE 42: Player #5 Blocks the Shots from Players #1, 2 and 6

ALTERNATE DEFENSE 3:2 FOR OFFENSE 4:2 USING A PRESSURE, DYNAMIC DEFENSE

Another way of defending against a 4:2 offense is to use a more dynamic approach. This approach rushes the players on offense and causes them to make mistakes – for example an inaccurate pass or a rushed shot. Using these tactics, you're players are focusing more on pressuring the offense than on blocking the shots as I described in the previous section. In order for these tactics to start, there should be a predetermined "visual cue/code". For example, a visual cue can be when a specific player is about to receive a pass in a man-down situation, your players should know what position to go to and how to behave. I will provide several variations in steps below.

The key to mastering these tactics is practice. These should be practiced over and over again until they become second nature. The figure below shows the movement of each player and her responsibilities for the two players she is covering.

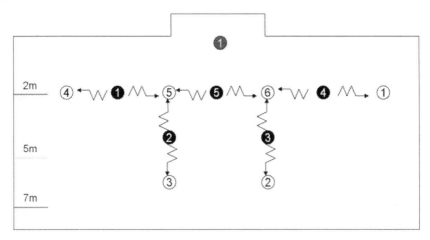

FIGURE 43: Dynamic Approach with Swimming to Press All Players/Movement of Players during Man-Down Dynamic Defense

FIRST APPROACH: DYNAMIC APPROACH WITH SWIMMING TO PRESS ALL PLAYERS

The first approach to the pressure dynamic defense is when your team pressures the five players closest to the ball, leaving the mirror opposite player open. In this way, you leave the furthest player from the ball without a defender, so that the ball must be passed to her. That forces the opposing team to make a hard pass, which they likely will miss. This gives our team at best the chance to steal, or at least buys us time to get in position for further defense. The offense also may feel rushed to take a shot, which is never a high percentage shot.

Like I said above, all players must know that the particular pass is the "visual cue/code" and therefore they have to react/swim to the positions that they are supposed to. If the players are late to get to their positions, the opposing team has enough time (doesn't feel rushed) to pass to some other player and the pressure we wished to create drops, which is the opposite effect of what we are trying to accomplish here. The purpose of this defense is to press all the players except the one in the opposite wing. This pass to the opposite wing is a hard pass to make and often players are coached not to pass to that player since it is hard to catch. Therefore we are counting on the ball hitting the water instead of the hand of the player and then having enough time to do the same drill but on the opposite side. Dropping the ball in the water gives the defense and the goalie enough time to get into their positions. Also, forcing the wing-to-wing passes makes the opposing team pass the ball over three of our players on defense (players #4, 5 & 1), which gives us a high probability for a steal to be made by these players. I recommend that the team uses a pass to the right wing (counting on the fact that the right wing player is a right-handed player) which will make this pass a difficult one to catch and hopefully make the wing player spend time handling the ball which also gives us more time to get to that player and make the foul.

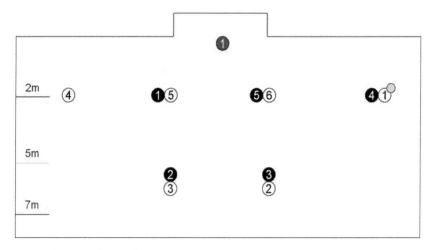

FIGURE 44: Visual Cue – the Ball is Passed to Player #1 and Defense Sets Up Immediately in Position. The Offense is Fully Covered so we are Forcing a "Rainbow" Pass (from Player #1 to Player #4)

For this first approach, the step by step actions are:

At the moment of the pass (while the ball is in the air) to player #1 on offense, defensive player #4 sprints towards the offensive player #1; defensive players #2 & 3 also sprint towards offensive players #2 & 3; defensive **player #5 – the center-defender** – sprints towards player #6; defensive player #1 sprints towards offensive player #5. After this transition of all players, the only player that's left open is the left wing player (#4) who is the furthest point away from the ball.

All defensive players have to play strict pressure defense and not allow the ball to be passed to the players that they are guarding. If and when the ball is passed to those pressed players, the defensive players MUST make the foul. Any time that the ball is passed to a covered player, your defensive player covering must make a foul until the ball is passed to the only open player; the opposite wing. At this point, only the 2 meter line defense switches towards the ball – defensive players #2 and 3 stick with their pressure defense, making the foul if the ball gets to them. This type of defense can be done until the shot clock runs out or it can only be done once, and be used as a surprise effect. Also, when a foul is committed on players #2 or 3, it can be replaced by the shot blocking stationary defense detailed in the section on *Defense 3:2 for Offense 4:2* on page 51. In this kind of dynamic approach to man-down defense, the goalie is in charge of blocking the shots for the whole cage, since the defense is busy swimming and won't be able to block shots.

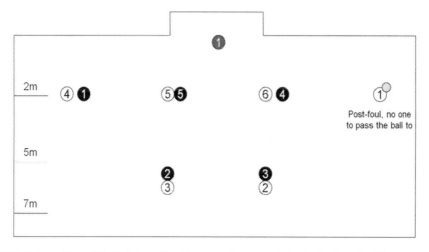

FIGURE 45: When Player #1 is Fouled, the Two Meter Line Defense Switches to the Opposite Side

SECOND APPROACH: DYNAMIC APPROACH WITH SWIMMING TO PRESS THREE PLAYERS

In this approach, instead of swimming to press five players as I explained above, the second approach is to swim to press three players – players #3, 4 & 5 – which is one side of the front court offense. The visual cue in this situation is the moment when one player on offense is about to get the ball. Typically it's player #1 or player #4 who receives the pass – and that is the moment for the defense to start this tactic. Here we are forcing a pass to the right side of the offense, which is relatively hard to catch and at the same time shoot a high percentage shot. On top of that, we have defensive player #2 in the passing lane between offensive player #4 and player #2. This tactic is implemented when we have one side of offense stronger than the other, and we don't want to allow the shot to be taken from the stronger side.

The idea is to press one side of the offense and force long, hard passes during which the goalie and the defense will have enough time to get set up. Needless to say that by forcing these long and hard passes we hope that offense drops the ball - or spends more time handling it - which goes hand in hand with letting the 20 second shot clock run out during the man-down for our team.

In Figure 46 below the visual cue is the pass to the left wing player (player #4). While the ball is in the air, defensive player #1 will sprint to press player #4 on offense; **defensive player #5 (the center-defender)** will press player #5 on offense; defensive player #2 will press player #3 on offense; defensive player #3 stays back on player #6 and presses; defensive player #4 stays back pressing player #6 and blocking the shot when the ball comes in possession of player #1 on offense.

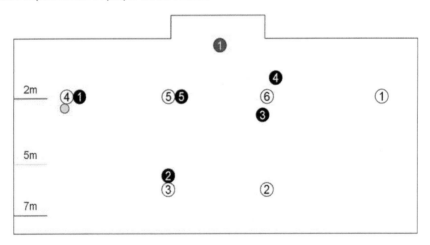

FIGURE 46: Pressing One Side of the Offense When Player #4 Receives the Pass

This tactic is used when the players on one side of the offense are much stronger than the other. We are implementing this tactic to rush the stronger, more skilled side and force shots and passes to the weaker side. When the ball is still passed to the stronger side, even though we pressed on defense in the manner shown above, it is important to make the foul as soon as possible. It is also necessary that everybody who went into transition (players #1, #5 & #2 on defense) remains pressuring the appropriate players until the ball is passed to the weaker (in this case right) side.

64

> *We are implementing this tactic to rush the stronger, more skilled side and force shots and passes to the weaker side.*

This defensive tactic can be repeated every time the ball is passed to the left wing (player #4) until the shot clock runs out, or it can be done once to make the other team feel rushed and make a bad decision by forcing the pass or the shot from the bad situation. If you use this tactic only once for a surprise effect, replace it with *Defense 3:2 for Offense 4:2* on page 51 when the ball is returned to the weaker side of the offense.

THIRD APPROACH: DYNAMIC APPROACH WITH SWIMMING TO PRESS THE BEST
SHOOTER

This type of defense is utilized when the offense has one very good player/shooter on their team who can't be left alone with the ball for too long. As the visual cue for this action we don't wait for the long pass to one of the wing players (like in the examples above), but we look for a pass that goes directly to that strong individual player (in this example player #3). As it's shown in the figure below, at the moment when player #3 gets the ball, defensive player #2 goes out to press this player and not leave her any space/time for a well situated shot. Every time that player #3 gets the ball, she is pressured but not fouled, as she is outside of the 5 meter line and could take a clean shot. After player #3 passes to one of her teammates, defensive player #2 goes back to guarding player #5 on offense until player #3 gets the ball again.

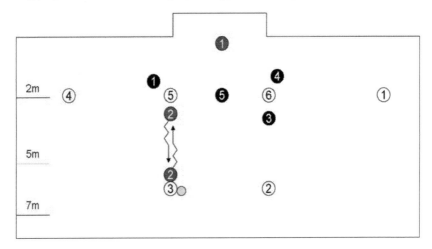

FIGURE 47: Player #3 is Pressed as Soon as She Gets the Ball

In this approach it is important that all defensive players understand their positioning for the stationary defense from section *Defense 3:2 for Offense 4:2* on page 51. It's important to note that when the player we are trying to block gets the ball, your defensive player should "scull" in the vertical position and block any potential shots. The goal of this spin on man-down defense is to set up the first line of defense at the 2 meter line to block the shots, and the second line of defense, at the 5 meter line, to pressure the player with the ball.

Referring to the figure below, at the moment of a pass to player #2 on offense, player #3 on defense goes out to pressure this player and make it hard for her to make a well-situated shot. When the ball is passed to player #3, defensive player #3 comes back and stays in front of player #6 on offense, and defensive player #2 presses offensive player #3. The whole thing repeats itself until the shot, block or steal is made. We use this type of defense on man-down when we don't want to leave enough time for offense to build the appropriate space and positioning that's necessary for a good shot opportunity for their two outside shooters, which is why we sprint to the person with the ball. If the ball is passed to one of the wings, we do not swim out and press them; instead the defensive players #1 & 4 will play stationary defense. During this action, **Player #5 – the center-defender - blocks outside shots in front of the cage.**

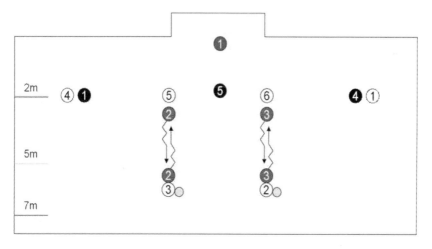

FIGURE 48: When One of the Two Outside Shooters Gets the Ball, Her Appropriate Guardian Will Press Her

FIFTH APPROACH: DYNAMIC APPROACH WITH SWIMMING TO PRESS ALL OUTSIDE SHOOTERS

As in the previous example, your defense is positioned in the same way – using sculling to get to the player with the ball, and setting themselves up in the stationary defense when their player doesn't have the ball.

It's the same strategy as the fourth approach above; but you are now involving your wing defenders. There is one caution – and that is that they should stagger their return and advance when the ball is passed. You don't want to have an open player on the post for an easy shot, so for example if player #2 has the ball, and she passes to player #1, then player #4 on defense has to wait to scull out to player #1 for player #3 on defense to come back and cover player #6 on the post.

In order for this to be successful, we need to have players who are good jumpers and fast scullers because it's much slower to get from point A to point B sculling than it is swimming.

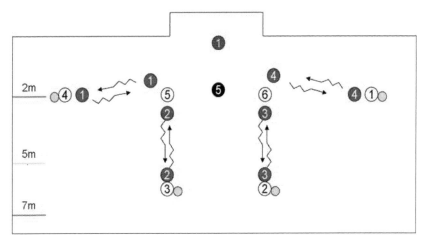

FIGURE 49: When Players #1, 2, 3 Or 4 Get the Ball, Their Appropriate Guardians Will Press Them

Umbrella Defense for 4:2 Offense

This is a modified umbrella defense that helps you get back quickly on the counterattack so you can score goals quickly. One part of this tactic is to play man-on-man defense on players #5 & 6, and the other part is to play zone defense on the outside players. Players #5 & 6 on offense are positioned on the 2 meter line on the posts, and are guarded by players #1 **and the center-defender, player #5.** The rest of the defense is positioned in between the outside players that together form the "umbrella" positioning. Defender #2 goes in between players #3 & 4 that are on offense; defender #3 goes in between players #3 & 2 that are on offense, and defender #4 goes in between players #1 & 2 that are on offense.

When you are behind a couple of goals, this is a strategy that you can use. It involves some risk, because the shooting lanes are wide open and no arms are up blocking the shots except from the players #1 & 5, but it is a great way to quickly go to counterattack after the team on offense misses the shot. Your team should have a 3 on 2 counterattack every single time. Defensive players #2, 3 & 4 – when they go on offense - will be up against offensive players #2 & 3 when they go on defense.

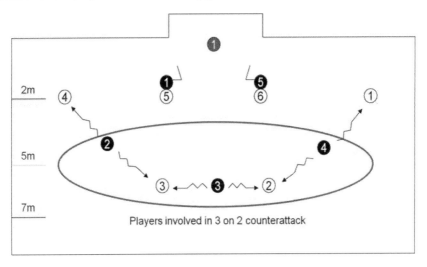

FIGURE 50: Umbrella Defense for Man-Down System 4:2

Defense 4:1 for offense 4:2

In this situation, defensive player #1 presses player #4 on offense; defensive player #2 presses player #5 on offense; defensive player #5 presses player #6 on offense, and defensive player #4 presses player #1 on offense. The only player who is in charge of two players is player #3, who positions herself in between players #3 & 2 on offense.

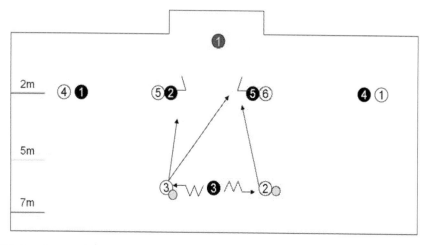

FIGURE 51: Defense 4:1 for Offense 4:2

Applying this tactic will force the defense to build a situation for the shot that comes from either player #3 or player #2. Defensive player #3 will swim in between the two top players, not letting them hold on to the ball for too long. If one of these two players (players on the 6 meter line) drops the ball, defensive player #3 will stay back primarily guarding the space in between players #2 & 3 and will not let the other top player (the one who didn't drop the ball) get inside of the 5 meter line. The reasoning for not making a foul and following the player who is outside 6-7 meter line is that she is not dangerous at that distance and because the better solution would be to let the shot clock run out.

No matter what happens, defenders have to press the first line (2 meter line) so that none of these players can get the ball. When player #3 on offense has the ball, defensive player #2 is in charge of blocking the closer-corner of the cage, and **defensive player #5, who is the center-defender**, blocks cross-cage shots; defensive player #3 swims in between the two top players. When player #2 on offense has the ball, defensive player #5 is blocking closer-cage shots, and defensive player #2 is blocking the cross-cage shots; defensive player #3 swims in between the two top players.

MAN-UP POWER PLAY

Since man-ups only last 20 seconds, these are fast paced maneuvers where the ball is passed to as many players as possible so that a gap in the defense is created. Ideally, each player should be in possession of the ball for 2 seconds tops and in that time she needs to catch, fake at least twice, and pass the ball.

Because water polo is played in the water which inhibits movements and forces players to move about four times slower compared to when on dry land, man-up situations are a big advantage for the team. The ball can travel much faster than the defense players can, therefore this creates an advantage in the game having one man-up because somebody will always stay alone and open for the pass or shot. This is why coaches pay special attention to this part of the game and spend a lot of time practicing different tactics to improve their team's man-up offense. The team that is more successful in this part of the game will be able to do much better compared to the team that is not skilled at converting the man-up situations into goals.

The main idea in man-up situations is to take advantage of having one more player in the water than the opposing team has. This means that the action needs to be designed in such manner so that the player who is not guarded gets the ball and shoots it at the part of the goal that is not being defended. This is done by passing the ball amongst the players, faking shots and sliding into the open space so that some other player gets freed up from the defense. While the ball is being passed around, the defense and the goalie have to react to this by moving in the direction of the ball flight. Because the flight of the ball is much faster than the players can actually swim or move otherwise, this creates a much desired advantage. The defense and the goalie will be late to get back to the player who is taking the shot and to defend the other part of the cage.

Before we go into positioning and individual tactics, it is important to say that ball handling skills are crucial in order to be successful during a man-up power play. Ball handling skills consist of passing, faking and shooting. When the player is faking she needs to have such a believable "fake" so that it will throw the defense and the goalie off, and not let them know when the ball is going to be released from the player's hand and in which direction it will go. The player's body language should not tell the defense nor the goalie whether that shot is going to be a lob shot, skip shot, direct shot, cross-cage shot, closer-cage shot, a pass, etc.

When you are in control of the ball during the man-up situation, you are in control of the situation. What this means is that the defense has to react to the system of play that you dictate as we explained in the man-down defense section. The most frequent systems of offense are immediate scoring, offense system 3:3, and offense system 4:2

Below I describe these different systems in more detail and provide suggestions on various possibilities for scoring. Since man-ups only last 20 seconds, these are fast paced maneuvers where the ball is passed to as many players as possible so that a gap in the defense is created. Ideally, each player should be in possession of the ball for 2 seconds tops and in that time she needs to catch, fake at least twice, and pass the ball.

IMMEDIATE SCORING ON MAN-UP

This type of play is something that is usually overlooked and not practiced at all, which is a big mistake. What happens is that the player in the hole stays open since her defender got kicked out. She then passes the ball securely and as quickly as possible outside to any player (making sure while doing this she is outside the 2 meter line), and then she gets the ball back immediately and scores. This double pass situation - like any other situation - needs to be broken down and practiced so that when the opportunity arises everybody knows what to do. When a player scores an easy goal like this it degrades the confidence of the opposing team, and enhances the mood and confidence of your team. They will swim with pride back to defense.

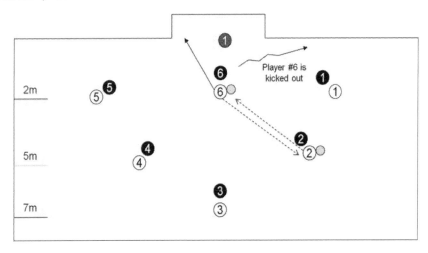

FIGURE 52: Immediate Scoring on Man-Up

OFFENSE SYSTEM 3:3

This figure shows the man-up offense set up in the formation of 3:3. We have three players at the 2 meter line (center and two wings) and three players on the 5-6 meter line set up in a slight curve, together forming an umbrella positioning that differs slightly from the regular umbrella (when we have an even number of players on offense and defense). The difference is that the wings are a little bit closer positioned. The reason for having wings a little closer to the cage is because we don't need to open up the space for the hole-man, since we will never pass the ball to her when we are on man-up; instead we will look for the shot coming from the players from the outside positions #2, 3, or 4. Below are some examples of where the shot can come from in defensive system 3:3.

73

For offense system 3:3, I will describe four possible maneuvers for scoring, all of which have your players set up in the 3:3 configuration. The figure below illustrates the beginning position of the 3:3 man-up offense, without the defense pictured.

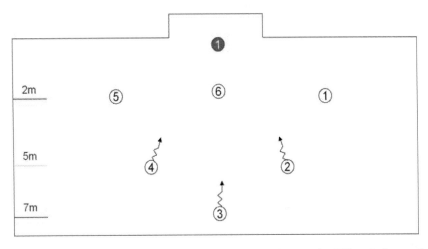

FIGURE 53: Systems of Man-Up Power Play in the Formation 3:3 – Basic Formation Without Defense and Potential Movement Toward the Goal

EXAMPLE 1: PLAYER #4 TAKES THE SHOT

In a man-up situation, every action should start with passing the ball around at least once to all three outside players (#2, 3, & 4) who will make two strong fakes while sliding forward and then pass to the next player. After the ball has circulated once or twice, the tactic is initiated by player #3 who moves forward while faking. At the moment that she is attacked by player #2 on defense, player #4 on offense has to use the open space and slide forward without the ball. Player #3 then passes the ball to player #4 at the last moment before she is attacked (which requires a high level of skill) because if she passes earlier, the defender #2 will not open up the space for player #4 on offense. As soon as player #4 gets the ball she needs to shoot (in the left corner-without faking), or after one fake she can shoot cross-cage. The action is prepared for player #4 by having the other players on offense fake when they get the ball – which exhausts the entire defense and

74

forces them to slide out of their positions so that they are not aligned with the posts that they are guarding. Because the defense is facing away from the goal, they cannot see the goal and the matching corners that they are supposed to guard. This is why it is common to see the "gaps" starting to appear in the defense after the ball is passed around for a little while. This is the reason why player #4 doesn't need to fake or needs to fake no more than once, because faking will waste time and allow the defense to adjust their positions and block the shot.

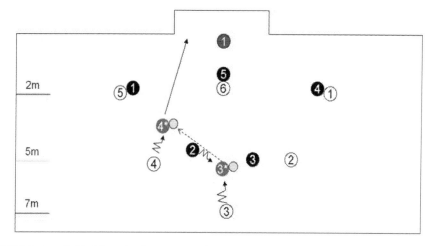

FIGURE 54: Example #1 - Where the Shot Can Come from in System 3:3

> *...it is common to see the "gaps" starting to appear in the defense after the ball is passed around for a little while.*

The same can be done when we have a left-handed player in position #2. Player #3 again opens up the space by moving forward, player #2 follows, gets the ball and shoots.

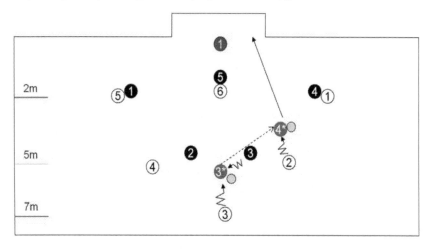

FIGURE 55: Example #1 – Another Option of Where the Shot Can Come from in System 3:3

EXAMPLE 2: PLAYER #3 TAKES THE SHOT

As before, this action begins with couple of passes amongst players #2, 3, & 4 before the tactic begins. After the ball has travelled around for a little bit, it will end up with player #3 who will slide forward while faking. This movement forward should be done as often as possible when on man-up since the closer the players get, the more likely they are to score. If player #3 is not attacked, she will get as close as she can and take a shot. The same can be done with players #2 & 4 when they are not guarded. This action may seem simple, but if the defense is not really committing to you, you should take advantage of it, and take your best shot at the cage.

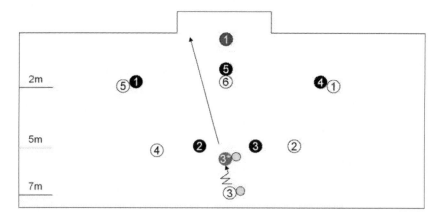

FIGURE 56: Example #2 - Where the Shot Can Come from in System 3:3

EXAMPLE 3: PLAYER #4 OR 2 TAKES THE SHOT

This action starts in the same way with the ball being passed around; trying to move the players on defense and tire them out. After this, player #3 will get the ball. She will move forward while faking and paying attention on where the defenders are going to attack (either from player #2 or from position #3). Depending on this, she will pass the ball to the player whose defender left her (either to player #2 or #4). So now, depending on who has the ball (#2 or #4), that player needs to move in even more with one or two fakes and pass to the opposite player (either player #2 or #4) who then takes the shot in the non-protected corner which for player #4 is the left corner and for player #2 the right corner. The action goes 3-2-4-shot (shown in the figure below) in the goalie's right or; 3-4-2-shot in the goalie's left corner. The second action (3-4-2-shot) is easier to accomplish if we have a left-handed player on position #2).

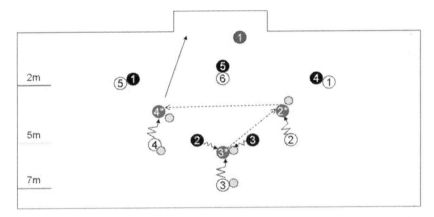

FIGURE 57: Example #3 - Player #4 or #2 Takes the Shot in System 3:3

Example 4: Players #3 or #4 take the shot

This tactic seriously begins with player #2 who will get players #3 & 4 open. The reason I say seriously is because a couple of passes need to be made amongst players #2, 3, & 4 before the tactic begins. After the ball had circulated around once or twice, player #2 needs to slide towards the right post while faking the shot and gluing the defense and the goalie to the right side. While player #2 is moving forward, the defender #3 will have to follow her, which will allow player #3 on offense to move in as well (without the ball). At the last moment before player #2 on offense gets attacked, she will pass the ball to player #3 who then will take the shot without faking at the goalie's right corner (because the goalie was at the opposite side of the cage). If player #2 on defense attacks player #3 on offense, player #3 will quickly pass without faking to player #4 who then takes a shot at the goalie's right corner. It's also possible that the pass goes directly from player #2 to player #4 depending where the defense is.

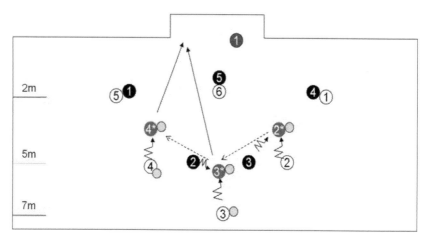

FIGURE 58: Example #4 - Players #3 or #4 Take the Shot in System 3:3

If the team has a left-handed player in position #2 this same action can be done from the opposite side. Player #4 goes in and passes to player #3 who then passes to player #2 who takes the shot in the goalie's left corner or straight from player #4 to player #2 and the direct shot at the same corner.

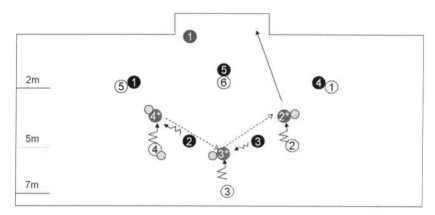

FIGURE 59: Example #4 - Player #2 Takes the Shot in System 3:3

OFFENSE SYSTEM 4:2

For offense system 4:2, I will describe several possible maneuvers for scoring, and give tactical ideas on which position the team can score from. The figure below illustrates the beginning position of the 4:2 man-up offense, without defense pictured.

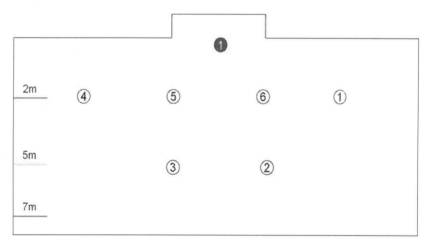

FIGURE 60: System 4:2 - Basic Positioning Without Defense

79

In the 4:2 system, we have four players in the first line (2 meters) and two in the second line (5 meters). Having four players in the first line makes it easier to score and harder to defend, so most advanced teams will play this tactic (system 4:2) more often. The players with the strongest legs should be positioned on the posts (players #5 & 6), and the strongest shooters should be positioned in positions #2 & 3. Each man-up situation should start with players getting in their positions (as shown in the figure above) as quickly as possible. Going from even numbers of players on both teams to man-up situation should be practiced repeatedly. What I mean is, that it is important to get in designated man-up positions as soon as possible. These positions are determined during practice time, and depend on coaches' decisions. Once the man-up starts and the players are positioned, all players can slide in all four directions (left, right, forward, backward) creating 3:3 system or some other system. This sliding of the players and the creation of different systems of the players is very important because it forces the defense to move out of their positions. This allows the offense to take advantage of now open trajectories for a pass or a shot.

Creation of these new systems lasts only for as long as it is necessary to finish a particular action. If the player who was supposed to shoot is not open, all players should return to the 4:2 system, and a new (or the same) action should start again. It's worth mentioning that the man-up situation lasts only 20 seconds, which makes it possible that the shooter we are trying to open will not get open. When that happens, the shot should not be forced, instead, we should look for another solution, even if the man-up situation expires, and the player who was kicked out returns to the field.

EXAMPLE 1: PLAYER #3 TAKES THE SHOT

Every action must start with passing the ball around once, to all four outside players (#1, 2, 3, 4) who will make two strong fakes and then pass to the next player – similar to what we had during system 3-3. After the ball has circulated amongst the outside players at least once, player #1 gets the ball and goes toward the goal line while faking and getting up high. The other outside players (#2, 3 & 4) slide to the right moving sort of like in a circle. Players #6 slides out from 2 meter line trying to get open and get the pass from player #1. If player #6 couldn't get open from the defender #3, player #1 will pass to player #2 who fakes once (towards goalie's left side) and passes to player #3 who takes the shot in the opposite corner (her left/goalie's right). If player #3 is open right away, the pass can go from player #1 to player #3 and the shot follows. This same action can be done by moving the offensive players to the left instead of to the right. Player #1 gets the ball, fakes and moves to the left, while players #2 & 3 also slide to the left. Pass goes from player #1 to player #2 to player #3 and the shot follows.

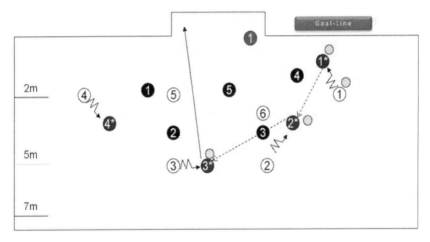

FIGURE 61: Example #1 - Player #3 Takes the Shot in System 4:2

Example 2: Player #4 takes the shot

After the ball had circulated around the outside players once, player #2 gets the ball and slides to the right and inward while faking and gluing the defense and the goalie to the right post. Her movement is being followed by players #3 & 4 who move as shown in the figure below. Player #2 passes the ball to player #3 who passes to player #4 who then shoots in the left corner (goalie's right) without faking. Player #4 can also shoot cross-cage after one fake. In addition, if player #4 is open beforehand, player #2 can directly pass to player #4 and skip the pass to player #3.

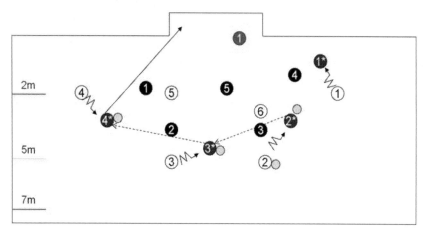

FIGURE 62: Example #2 - Player #4 Takes the Shot in System 4:2

EXAMPLE 3: PLAYER #2 TAKES THE SHOT

As always, the ball has to circulate around the four outside players before the actual tactic starts. After that, player #1 gets the ball and goes towards the goal line trying to glue the defense and the goalie to the right side of the goal/field. During this shift of player #1, the other outside players (#2, 3, & 4) also slide from their original positions to the right side (as shown in the figure). Player #1 passes the ball to player #2 who takes the shot in the opposite corner (left) without faking.

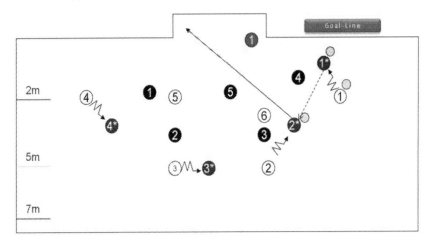

FIGURE 63: Example #3- Player #2 Takes the Shot in System 4:2

EXAMPLE 4: PLAYER #1 TAKES THE SHOT

Like I said before, every time we have a man-up situation the ball is being passed around from player to player before the tactical part can start. After the ball is passed around once, player #3 will get the ball, fake hard, and then slide to the left and inward, with the idea to glue the goalie to the left post. At the same time, players #1 & 2 will also slide to the left and fill up the space created by the sliding of player #3. Player #3 will quickly pass the ball to player #2, who passes to player #1, who then takes the shot in the right corner without faking, or shoots cross-cage after one fake. This action is pretty advanced for beginners, but can be done with novice players if there is a left-handed player in position #1. On the other hand, if we have an advanced team that we are coaching, player #1 can be right-handed, but she would have to be very skilled, and goalie must be significantly out of position. Also, notice how player #6 on offense slides out from being on the post, to the wing position at the same time as all other player movement is happening.

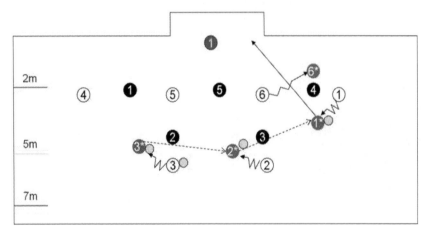

FIGURE 64: Example #4 - Player #1 Takes the Shot in System 4:2

EXAMPLE 5: PLAYER #1 TAKES THE SHOT – ALTERNATE APPROACH

The action starts after the ball has circulated around the outside players at least once in the same manner I described in previous examples. Then, player #4 gets the ball and she starts sliding towards the goal-line, and fakes the goalie to the left post. At the same time players #1, 2, & 3 are following the same movement (to the left) and taking advantage of the shifted defense. Player #4 passes to player #1 who takes the shot in the right corner (goalie's left) without faking, or shoots cross-cage after one fake. This is a good play for the left-handed player or a skilled right-handed player who can catch that pass easily and get in shooting position quickly. The same combination is possible on the other side, which is appropriate for beginners and intermediate teams (passes from player #1 to player #4).

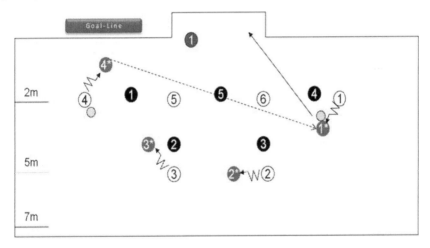

FIGURE 65: Example #5 - Player #1 Takes the Shot in System 4:2 – Alternate Approach

EXAMPLE 6: PLAYER #5 TAKES THE SHOT

This action starts after the ball has circulated amongst the outside players who made 2 fakes with getting up high and gluing the defense and the goalie in each ball possession. When the ball is passed to player #1, she will start going towards the goal-line and towards the cage. Her movement is being followed identically by player #5. Players #4 & 6 are moving in the opposite way from players #1 & 5 (they are sliding out to the 3 meter line). Every movement in this action is happening at the same time. That means that players #2 & 3 are moving as well, and that they are in sync with the other offensive players. All outside players are moving to the right, following player #1. The ball will be passed from player #1 to player #5 who will put the ball in the left corner of the cage (goalie's right). By breaking the first line of defense from being straight to being zigzag (we do it by moving players #4 & 6 in one direction, and players #1 & 5 in the opposite

85

direction), and sliding of players #2 & 3 we have a greater chance to score in the man-up situation.

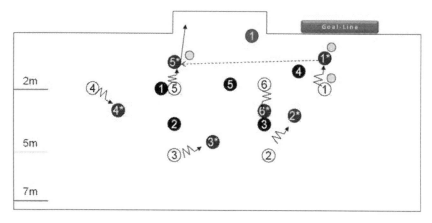

FIGURE 66: Example #6 - Player #5 Takes the Shot in System 4:2

EXAMPLE 7: PLAYER #6 TAKES THE SHOT

The action starts when the ball had gone around once. Player #1 gets the ball and goes towards the goal-line. Basically same thing happens as in the previous example, except when the defense doesn't cover player #6, she gets the ball from player #1 and shoots cross-cage. Remember that in example #3 above (Figure 63) I showed player #2 on offense getting the ball and taking the shot. These two drills should be practiced together; whichever player is open will take the shot.

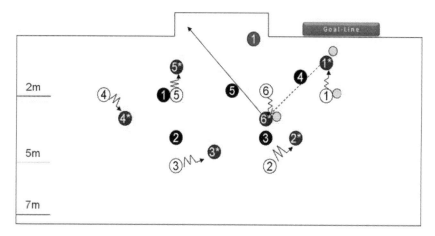

FIGURE 67: Example #7 - Player #6 Takes the Shot in System 4:2

Example 8: Player #4 takes the shot

After the ball has circulated once around the players, player #1 gets the ball and goes towards the goal-line while faking. Players #2 & 3 are sliding to the right following player #1. Player #4 goes from the 2 meter line to the 3 meter line moving towards the goal and to the right side, opening a better shooting lane for herself. At the same time, player #5 is following player #1 going practically towards the cage and staying aligned with player #1. Players #1 & 5 are in the same line, while player #6 is moving from the 2 meter line to the 3 meter line, still staying aligned with the post. During this time, he remains aligned with player #4. Player #1 passes the ball to player #4 who takes the shot in the left corner (goalie's right). Movements of players #5 & 6 are very important, because, when the first line of offense gets crooked, the defense has much harder time defending the cage.

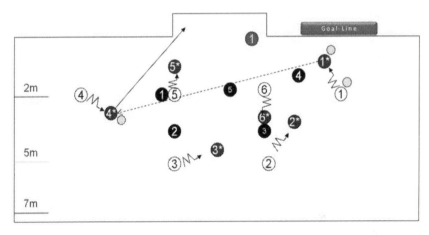

FIGURE 68: Example #8 - Player #4 Takes the Shot in System 4:2

EXAMPLE 9: PLAYERS #5 OR #6 TAKE THE SHOT

After the ball has circulated amongst four outside players, player #2 gets the ball and fakes the goalie to the right post. She then passes to player #5 who takes the shot without faking in the opposite, left corner (goalie's right).

The same tactic can be done on the other side if the team has a left-handed, or a highly skilled player in position #6 to tip the ball in the cage. Player #3 gets the ball and starts faking the goalie to the left post; she then passes to player #6 who takes the shot in the opposite, right corner (goalie's left).

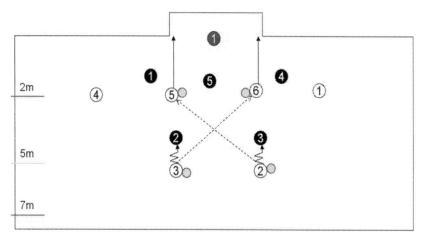

FIGURE 69: Example #9 Players #5 or 6 Take the Shot in System 4:2

EXAMPLE 10: PLAYER #5 TAKES THE SHOT

After the ball is passed around once, player #4 will get the ball and fake the goalie and the defense to the left post. At the same time players #2 & 3 slide to the right forcing the defense to follow them. Also, player #6 moves in following the movement of player #4 on offense. Now, if player #5 is not properly guarded, player #4 can pass the ball to player #5, who will with tip the ball away. Player #5 is sliding out a little bit, just enough to get separated from defensive player #5. The reason why player #5 won't slide out more, like we had in previous examples, is because it is pretty challenging to tip the ball behind the goalie from further away, especially because player #5 in this example is a right-handed player. This pass needs to be high, so that player #5 has to get up high in order to get to it. The shot that player #5 is taking is a shot with tips of the fingers and player #5 needs to face player#4 and point her right shoulder toward the cage so that she is ready to make a quick shot tipping the ball in the closer-corner and surprising the goalie. Player #6 on offense is there in case there is a rebound.

When we have a left-handed player in this position, this action is much easier to accomplish, and in that scenario player #5 on offense can slide out more from the post – to the 3 or 4 meter line.

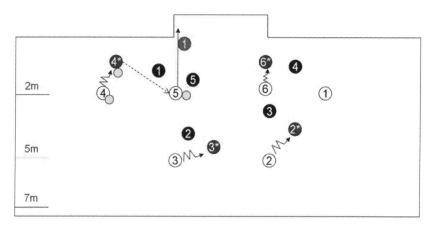

FIGURE 70: Example #10 - Player #5 Takes the Shot in System 4:2

I believe I have thoroughly explained the tactics you should use during any man-up situation. Control of the ball is crucial, since you only have a 20 second advantage to get your team in position to take a high percentage shot.

BREAKING ZONE DEFENSE

In order for the zone to be broken, players need to be very "water polo literate" and be able to recognize what kind of zone defense is being utilized. Once they have this knowledge, then they can break the zone defense statically (making crisp, precise passes and taking shots), or dynamically (driving or setting picks).

In order to conquer the space in front of her and break the zone defense, the player on offense must understand that the zone defense is responsible for protecting the space in front of the goal as well as blocking the area in the goal. In this way, zone defense assists the goalie.

TYPES OF ZONE DEFENSE

Below I am going to describe what kinds of zone defense can be used, so I can then prepare your offensive line to effectively break them. Understanding what the defense is doing will help the team on offense be one step ahead. We have four types of zone defense:

M-Zone Defense

This type of play is defined by neutralizing the center player completely by positioning the top driver defender (player #3) in front of the center, while two outer players #2 & 4 are positioned in between the three outside players as shown in the figure. This defensive tactic is good for producing counterattacks, but can be dangerous if there are good shooters in offensive positions #2, 3 or 4.

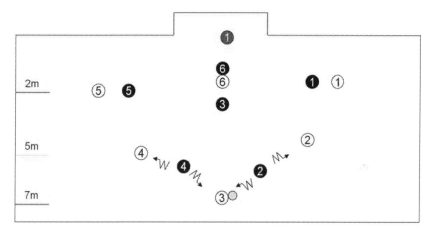

FIGURE 71: M-Zone Defense

SHALLOW ZONE DEFENSE

This type of defense requires letting your defensive line stay back in front of the hole-man – not swimming out to defend individual players. The offensive players are able to take shots from outside without being attacked, but, as a trade off, the defense is in control of the space in front of the center and parts of the goal with their arms up blocking shots. So, the defense is not going out to press the player with the ball; they stay back blocking the shots and preventing the ball from being passed into the hole. I use this defense when I have a stellar goalie and a strong blocking team.

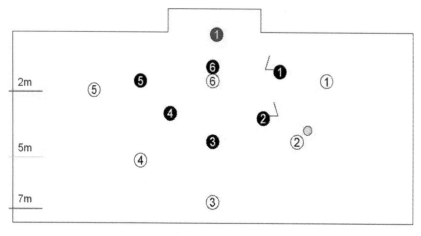

FIGURE 72: Shallow Zone Defense

JUMPING ZONE DEFENSE

This type of defense requires inhibition of the player with the ball (going out at her), while the other players are slightly backed up in the zone paying attention to the center player and the space in front of her. So as soon as one player gets the ball she'll be attacked. On the other hand as soon as she passes the ball, she'll be sloughed from and some other player will be attacked.

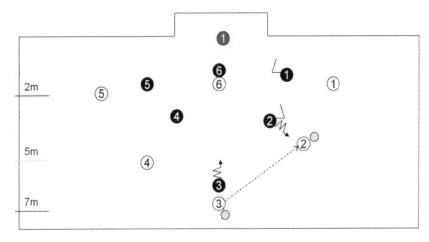

FIGURE 73: Jumping Zone Defense

COMBINED ZONE DEFENSE

This type of defense requires elements of both jumping and shallow zone defense. When using this defense, the coach determines which players the defense will pressure and attack when they are in possession of the ball, and which players will not be attacked. Instead of attacking the player with the ball, certain players will remain back in front of the center blocking shots, and preventing the ball from being passed to the hole-man, player #6. In the figure bellow, we have defensive players 2 & 3 playing jumping zone defense, while players 1, 4 & 5 play shallow zone defense.

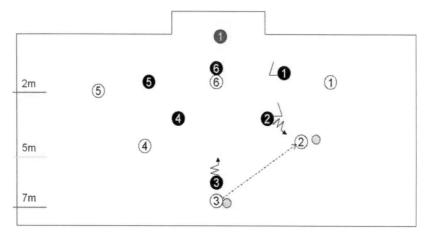

FIGURE 74: Combined Zone Defense

Below I am going to describe what steps the offense needs to take in order to break the zone defense. This information will help the coaches and players realize the minute details that are often overlooked and insufficiently practiced.

> *Each element of the game should be practiced separately and later put into the bigger picture.*

Methods to Break Zone Defense

In the next section I provide multiple detailed examples of breaking the zone defense. Most of the examples use shallow zone defense because it's easier to depict offense versus defense. However, each of these examples can be used to break any of the four kinds of zone defense described above.

Example 1

Just like we had in man-up situations in the systems 3:3 or 4:2, in order to score and break zone defense, the players need to pass and fake. By passing the ball amongst the outside players, we can force the goalie to move from one corner of the cage to the other. By faking before we make the pass we will force the goalie to stay glued to one post and make it difficult for her to get to the other side in time to make a save. In the figure bellow, we have a shallow zone defense that we want to break. Player #3 is sliding towards the open space while faking, from there, being closer to the goal, she can either pass to player #2 or 4, or she can take the shot. Player #3 has to be careful and not get blocked by the arms of the players that are on defense. Having the skill to successfully fake (tire out the goalie and defense), and see through the defense's tactics is necessary to be successful when breaking zone defense. Faking and quickly passing to the other player is a required skill that each player must possess in order to play serious water polo and be able to break zone defense.

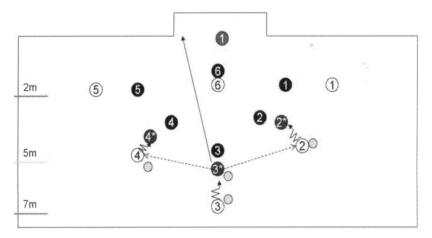

FIGURE 75: Example #1: Quick Passing and Shooting to Break Zone Defense

EXAMPLE 2

In this situation we also have a shallow zone defense that we want to break. In order to do so, player #3 will drive through and quickly slide out into the left wing. At the same time players #4 & 5 will have to slide out opening the space for the pass into the hole. If player #3's drive does not open up the hole, another player should drive. As the shot clock runs out and the zone defense gets broken, players #2 & 4 can shoot from outside positions or the ball can be passed into the hole. In the figure below we have player #2 pass the ball to player #4 who takes the shot – other solutions are also possible. Faking and moving while taking the shot is desirable trait in order to be successful at tiring the defense, goalie and scoring.

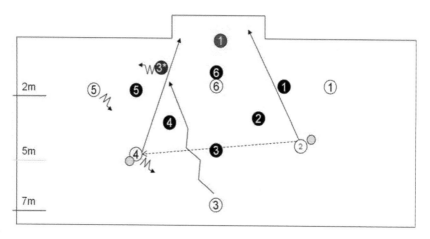

FIGURE 76: Example #2: Driving and Shooting from Outside to Break Zone Defense

EXAMPLE 3

In order to break the zone defense in this example we will take the shot from outside. The hypothesis is after we score a couple of times the other team's coach will order the team to stop sloughing from the outside players in order to better cover the shooters. This will open up the hole-man, and we can say that we broke the zone defense. In order to score, our team needs to make crisp accurate passes and to successfully fake which will tire up the goalie and glue her to the player who was faking. In the figure bellow player #3 is moving forward while faking and passes the ball to player #2 who is also moving forward while faking and glues the goalie to the right post. From there the ball is passed quickly to player #4 who was moving forward without ball and now takes the shot without faking in the left corner.

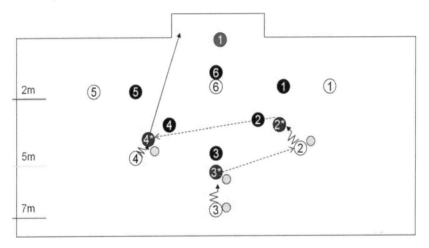

FIGURE 77: Example #3: Quick Passes and Shots to Break Zone Defense

Example 4

By passing the ball amongst the outside players, we can force the goalie to move from one corner of the cage to the other. By faking before we make the pass we will force the goalie to stay glued to one post and make it difficult for her to get to the other side in time to make a save. The action goes like this: player #1 fakes a shot into the right corner and passes the ball to player #4 who fakes while moving to the left side and passes to player #5 who fakes while moving toward the goal line gluing the goalie and the defense to the left side and passes to player #1 who had moved a little to the left side so that she has a better angle for the shot. Player #1 will take the shot in the right corner only if the shot is open, if it's not open she will pass the ball around again maybe trying to repeat the same tactics or will try something new if the team had practiced. This is an advanced drill to accomplish successfully, since it involves the pass from wing to wing, which is a hard pass to catch (especially from left wing to right wing).

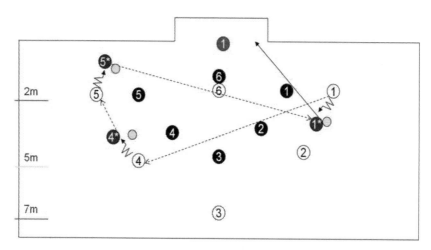

FIGURE 78: Example #4: Breaking Zone Defense By Sliding and Faking he Defense

EXAMPLE 5

In this example we are breaking the zone defense by setting the double hole-man offense. Player #6 on offense has to move to the right post, player #5 assumes the left post position. Player #4 on offense goes to the left wing and player #2 & 3 align themselves up with the posts. The ball goes from player #3 to player # 4 who is in the wing position, who then can either take a shot or can pass it to one of the centers. By having these two centers positioned at the 2 meter mark in front of the cage, we have made our team more dangerous for the defense to guard. Instead of the usual tactics of sloughing in front of the center player, the defense has to watch two center players now. We know that lots of kick outs are drawn from playing defense on the center position, so having two centers doubles your chance of a kick out, and if you are successful in putting the ball in the hole, it increases your chances for an easy shot.

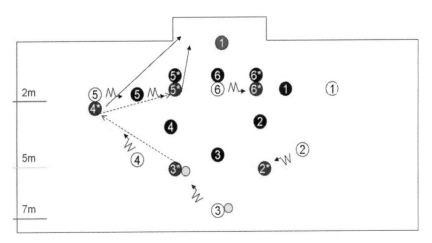

FIGURE 79: Example #5 - Breaking Zone Defense By Setting the Hole with Two Centers

EXAMPLE 6

In this situation, we have jumping zone defense, which is pressuring the player with the ball, the offense has a lot of space to break the zone by swimming and setting picks. When player #3 on offense gets the ball from player #4, she'll be attacked by her defender; at this moment defender #4 will drop back (since the player she was guarding doesn't have the ball anymore) to double team the hole-man together with defender #2. At the same time, player #4 on offense will sprint inside water and player #3 will pass the ball to player #2 and slide to the left where she won't get blocked by defender #3 if she gets the ball back and decides to shoot. Also, players #1 & 2 on offense can set the pick and try to get open for a shot. What we don't want to happen is to have player #4 drive in, and just sit in front of the goal being in the way. Player #4 should slide out of the way if she doesn't get the ball, so that area isn't overcrowded. Possible shots can come from players #1, 2, 3 or 4.

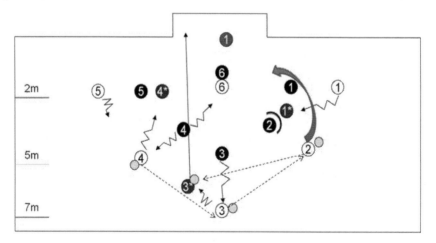

FIGURE 80: Example #6 - Breaking Zone Defense Example with Driving, Setting Picks and Shooting

Example 7

In this situation, the defense is playing M zone as it's shown in the figure above, the offense has the great opportunity to drive toward the goal. The inside water space is open and it is the easiest way to get advantage on the opponent. Players #2 & 4 on offense should sprint towards the right and left post respectively to get open for an easy shot. If this doesn't work out and players #2 & 4 didn't get the pass, they should slide out in the wing positions and now players #5 & 1 will take their place and drive again.

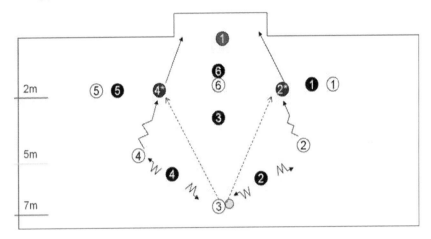

FIGURE 81: Example #7 - Breaking Zone Defense By Swimming Inside of the Perimeter from Both Sides

EXAMPLE 8

The goal of this play is to break the shallow zone defense through a combination of driving and setting picks. Even though this can possibly be done all at once, it is too difficult to visualize in a single figure so I will show each of these individual elements in two separate figures.

When player #2 has the ball and her defender is sloughing off of her, player #2 will fake the shot while moving toward the goal, at the very last moment before she gets attacked from her defender she will pass to player #1. As soon as the pass is made player #2 will sprint towards the left post trying to get open or to pick up her defender in order to free up the space in front of the hole. If she gets open she will get the ball from player #1 and take the shot on cage. If the zone is broken the ball goes in the hole. If neither of these two possibilities happens more action and movement is necessary.

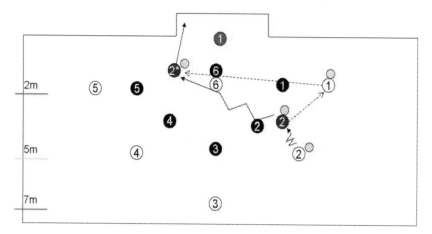

FIGURE 82: Example #8 - Swimming Inside the Perimeter to Break Zone Defense, Part 1

If defender #3 is too far back double teaming the center, just as defender #2 was, player #3 on offense will slide closer looking for the pass from player #1 to shoot.

At the same time players #5 & 4 will try to set the pick. The center player has to be turned towards player #1 on offense because she has the ball. Player #1 is moving toward the goal waiting for the perfect opportunity to pass to either the center player (#6) if the zone is broken, player #2 who might have gotten open (in the figure above), player #3 who might have been left alone, or player #4 or #5 who got themselves open by setting the pick. This is a good drill to practice to keep the team moving and creates multiple opportunities to shoot.

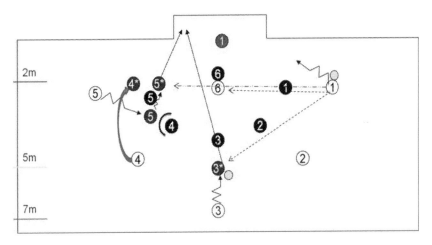

FIGURE 83: Example #8 - Setting Picks and Taking Shots to Break Zone Defense, Part 2

I trust I presented enough solutions to break the zone defense which is omnipresent in the water polo of today. It's possible for the center-defender (player #6) to be kicked out easily unless you're playing zone defense. If the center-defender doesn't pressure the hole-man, the hole-man will score an easy goal. So, as a solution for prevention of easy goals and numerous kick-outs, the zone defense found its place in most coaches' tactics.

> *I want to underline that taking shots from outside is usually perceived as easier tactic to implement in order to break the zone defense, but in reality is much harder.*

The reason for this is that the shot needs to be prepared by sliding of the player who is taking the shot as well as by sliding of the whole team – and this is high-level water polo tactic. Needless to say, shots from 5-8 meter line are very hard to score because of the distance, blocks and the presence of a decent goalie. The easier tactic to implement is to break the zone defense dynamically instead of statically. This is accomplished by driving inside of the perimeter. This tactic should be a primary tactic with young players and even with professional players. It would also add to the attractiveness and the popularity of the sport.

When building a team the coach has to plan every element of the game. That means having a fully stocked arsenal. As coach, you must develop your team to have two to three possible tactics for man-up, man-down, counterattack, defense against counterattack, breaking pressure defense, breaking zone defense etc. This approach requires a lot of practice and making sure that every player knows what to do in every single situation. When building a young, or JV team, one tactic per each part/category of the game is enough. The older the players are, the more time they have spent in the pool and therefore the more skills they should have. I think the most important part of coaching is to connect all parts of the game into one, so that the game is fluid and continuous. What I mean by that is to practice not only man down separately from counterattack separately from defending from counterattack, but to create a drill that will last for 3 transitions and will encompass man-down and then transition from man-down to counterattack, and then transition from counterattack to defending from counterattack. This is big picture water polo. After going deep into little details, you have to pull back and let the athletes play naturally and continuously.

BREAKING PRESSURE DEFENSE

In previous sections, I described solutions for breaking zone defense and now I will give suggestions for how to break pressure defense. By breaking pressure defense I mean getting open by yourself or with the help of one teammate and scoring a goal. I already described the RB technique for getting open and I touched on the driving technique as well. So in this chapter I'll focus a little more on setting picks as a tool for breaking pressure defense and I'll give a couple of driving examples as well.

There are many ways to set a pick in order to free up a player. In this section, I describe a few key tactics.

DRIVING TOWARDS THE CLOSER POST

Player #4 on offense drives toward the left post and in this example she is able to beat her defender. When player #4 is faster than her defender and is able to get inside water, she will get the ball from player #2 and will take the shot. The pass can come from either player #1, 2, 3 or 6 as long as player #2 is right-handed. This pass should only be made if player #2 had beaten her defender, otherwise the offense should continue trying to open some other player.

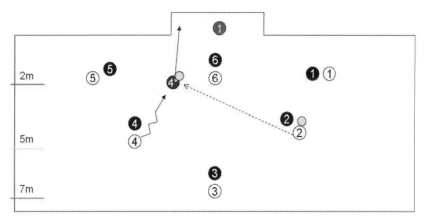

FIGURE 84: Driving Towards the Closer Post

105

HOLE-MAN BLOCKS THE DRIVER'S DEFENDER (PLAYER #6 BLOCKS PLAYER #2'S DEFENDER)

Player #3 has the ball and passes to player #1 (the action can start any other way as well). Player #6 will look to make a block (set a pick) on the defender #2 when player #2 starts driving diagonally towards the left post. Players #3, 4, and 5 have to slide out as it's shown in the figure below, and leave enough space for this block to be successful. After the confusion is made in that two defenders #2 & 6 are guarding player #6, player #2 should stay alone, get the pass from player #1 and take the shot. The ball is passed from player #3 to player #1 to player #2 and then the shot is taken. The passing can go any other way as well as long as player #2 can easily catch it.

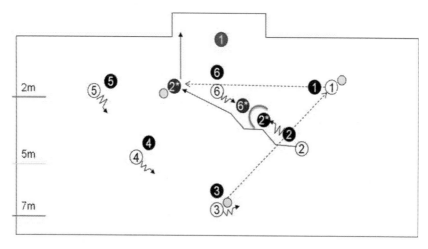

FIGURE 85: Hole-Man Blocks the Driver's Defender (Player #6 Blocks Player #2's Defender)

HOLE-MAN BLOCKS THE DRIVER'S DEFENDER WITH DEFENSE CALLING A SWITCH (PLAYER #6 BLOCKS PLAYER #2'S DEFENDER)

In this example we have the same situation as shown in the previous example with one little difference - that is, defender #6, who previously was guarding the center player, will switch and guard player #2 on offense after the block is made. Player #2 will slide out in the left wing and player #6 will be inside water with the defender on her back. After player #6 has made the block on defender #2, she will crash towards the right post looking for the pass and making sure she is not to be caught inside 2 meter line. She will then get the ball from player #1 and take the shot.

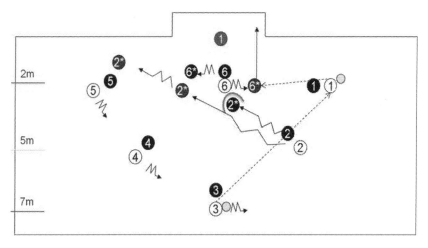

FIGURE 86: Hole-Man Blocks the Driver's Defender with Defense Calling a Switch (Player #6 Blocks Player #2's Defender)

Wing Sets the Pick on the Driver (Player #5 Blocks Player #4's Defender)

A good moment for setting picks is when the whistle is blown/or is about to be blown for an ordinary foul. One more thing to know is that the player on whom the pick is set should not be aware of your intentions (she should have her back turned to the player who is setting the pick). Wing player on offense #5 will set the pick on the defending player #4. Player #4 on offense will sprint around her teammate (player#5) and towards the left post, get the ball from player #3 or any other player on whom the foul was made. In order for this drill to work we have to assume that defenders #4 & 5 on defense will not switch their defenders, but instead, will be sticking to the original numbers they were guarding. This can happen especially in the younger categories. It is also useful to say that even though the figure shows that the pass is coming from #3, the ball can come from any position except from players #4 & 5 since they are involved in the action itself.

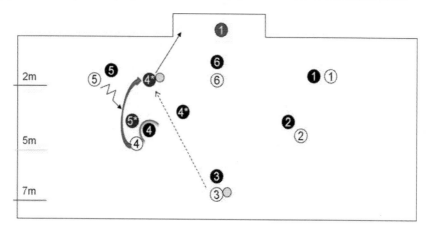

FIGURE 87: Wing Sets a Pick on the Driver (Player #5 Blocks Player #4's Defender)

Wing Sets the Pick on the Driver with Defense Calling a Switch (Player #5 Blocks Player #4's Defender)

This example is the same as the one shown above but with one difference. Defenders #4 & 5 will make the switch, as the more experienced players would do. So, player #5 will make the block on the defender #4, after which player #4 will crash towards the left post. Now, player #4 will be picked up by the defender #5 and when that happens, she needs to slide out into the left wing as soon as possible. Player #5 on offense will find herself in front of player #4 on defense (since she made the block on her). So, player #5 will have inside water advantage against defender #4. Player #5 has to crash towards the cage expecting the pass at any moment. The pass should come from player #3 because it's easy to catch, but it can come from any other positions as long as it doesn't involve the players who are setting picks. It's worth mentioning that center player (#6) should slide out towards the right post to leave enough space for player #5.

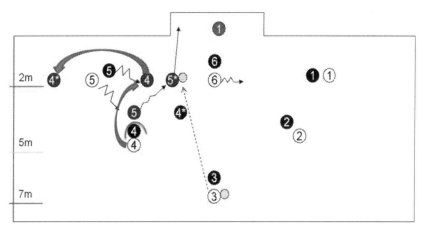

FIGURE 88: Wing Sets a Pick on the Driver with Defense Calling a Switch (Player #5 Blocks Player #4's Defender)

Right driver sets a pick on the left driver's defender (Player #2 Blocks Player #4's Defender)

Player #2 will swim across the field towards the defender #4 on whom she will make the block. As soon as the block is made, player #4 on offense will swim around the block and, if open, will get the ball from player #3. In order for this drill to work we have to assume that defender #2 will not switch her from player # 2 to player #4 on offense. Player #4 can also drive towards the right post instead of the left post. Both variations should be practiced.

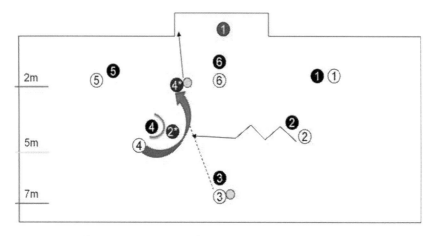

FIGURE 89: Setting a Pick in Between Two Drivers (Player #2 Blocks Player #4's Defender)

LEFT DRIVER #4 SETS A PICK ON LEFT WING #5'S DEFENDER

Player #4 on offense will set the pick on defender #5. Player #5 on offense will sprint around the block and get in the better position for shooting. The pass should come from player #2 after which the shot will be taken. Player #5 on offense should move toward the goal as much as she can since she is more likely to score from close up.

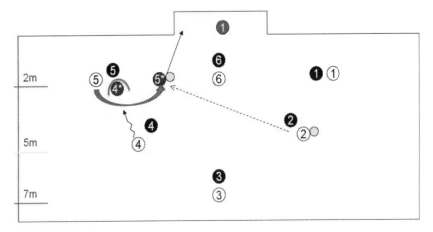

FIGURE 90: Left Driver #4 Sets a Pick on the Left Wing #5's Defender

Driving Toward The Left Post Following A Strong Vertical Jump

Player #4 (or any other outside player who has the ball) passes the ball into the hole and sprints towards the left post. Her job is to beat her opponent and stops at the 2 meter line by making a strong vertical jump waiting for the pass from player #6 who got a foul in the meantime and now will pass to an open player (in this example player #4). This drill can be done after a pass is made to any player in the field, and the drive can come from any position as well.

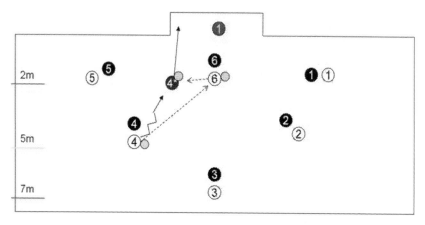

FIGURE 91: Driving Toward the Left Post Following a Strong Vertical Jump

Driving Across To the Further Post

Player #2 will sprint in front of the center going towards the left post. During this drive, similarly to any other driving, players have to even themselves out, to fill up the hole made with the absence of player #2 who was driving. Therefore, players #3, 4 & 5 will slide out to even themselves out and to create more space for player #2, so that she has more space to work with and doesn't get double teamed. If the drive is not successful, player #2 can slide out in the left wing. Hopefully, player #2 will gain the advantage on her defender and get ahead of her so that she can get the pass from player #3 or somebody else on the right side (if player #2 is right-handed). It's worth mentioning that this drill only works under the assumption that player #2 beats her opponent while swimming in.

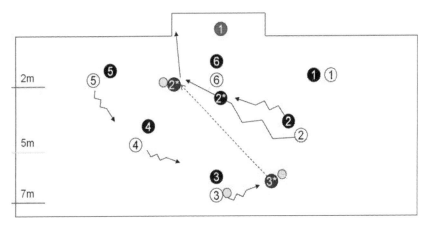

FIGURE 92: Driving Across to the Further Post

I believe that I have picked apart the game of water polo, dissecting it into the tiniest details and explaining those parts and giving ideas on how to practice each individual detail. The more details we recognize, the more water polo literate we are, and hopefully we as coaches and players will take time to think about these details and practice them.

CONCLUSION

It takes a special kind of individual to be a water polo player. What comes with the job is that you have to be able to take it. It takes getting yelled at on a daily basis from the coaches. It takes wanting a structured life and being a true team player. It takes being great on defense and great on offense – because you have both jobs. It takes being ready to get beaten up in the pool by opponents (who rarely get called for it because the referee almost never sees it). After you get beaten up you have to come back for some more and so it goes on and on. It takes wanting to be broken down and built up again every time you change the coach until the end of the competitive career. It takes swimming up and down the pool with your head up and an opponent on your back, as you chase the player that got away from your teammate. To the uninitiated, it seems like a terrible way to spend a few hours.

And yet, despite all of these challenges, the adrenaline rush of playing water polo well is second to none.

Similarly, being a coach is also a thankless job. You have to have the patience of a saint with the kids who often want to spend more time goofing off than listening to you. You can't back down, because even though they don't know it yet, they will be a better person for learning what you will teach them. You have to be ready to have your players not just hate, but sometimes despise you. You have to be a leader to the student athletes and a people person with them and their parents. You have to stand up to the ref, even though he might be a friend of yours. You have to manage different personalities on your team. You have to organize practices, tournaments, transportation, schedules; all of the details are up to you.

But seeing your players achieve greatness, even for a second, makes it all worth it.

Surprisingly, there are very few spectators at even the highest level college match. There are a few reasons for this; it's hard to understand the rules if you haven't played, it's hard to see what's happening because of all the splashing, which obscures what's happening below the water -- because much of the excitement occurs where the eye can't reach. Here on the East Coast, when you tell a neighbor that you coach or play water polo, they may look at you with a quizzical look. It's just not a sport that lends itself to being a spectator sport yet, even though it is the oldest Olympic team sport. In order to make water polo a more attractive sport for the audience, I suggest the changes to the game rules by making the fields shorter, instead of shortening the shot clock (like it's being proposed).

114

Right now, players have only 30 seconds (in most cases) to swim down the pool, set up the offense and score. They will spend approximately 15-20 seconds getting down to the other end of the pool depending on the age and level of play and then they are left with 10-15 seconds to organize the offense. In basketball, players *run* the similar distance (compared to the water polo court) which leaves them with 25 seconds to set up the offense. This is why I agree with efforts to make the game more popular and exciting by shortening the field and not the shot clock. The reasoning for this is that it will take approximately the same time to set up the offense (transitioning) in water polo as it takes in other team sports (basketball, soccer, European handball).

I believe that Water Polo is one of the healthiest sports for people to participate in because it is played in water, where there is no impact on the joints. Also, it is one of the best sports to be involved in because it is both a team and a contact sport which builds friendships for life. Finally, Water Polo is one of the best sports for building character because you depend on your teammates to cover your back and very often the game involves dragging an opponent on your back while you are chasing your teammate's escaped player down the length of the pool. It's no wonder why Navy Seals are using and promoting Water Polo as a key element in admission into their program.

In terms of the elements of the game of water polo (offense, defense, man-up, man-down) every player must constantly have in mind what *was* going on, what *is* going on and what *is supposed to happen* in the future (in terms of tactics). Every part of the game has to be practiced, discussed, and indeed perfected. Every player in the pool has a role to play and has to play it weather she does or does not have the ball.

The players have to know each other's strengths and weaknesses, and they also have to know what the coach expects from them. Often, players with less experience will try to do something that they have seen at some other match, but that element hasn't been approved by the coach nor practiced by the whole team. This is undesirable for team unity, because if everyone starts implementing unpracticed moves, it would lead to anarchy.

Every time a goal is scored, it should be seen as something that the whole team did together, not as something that only one player accomplished. When the player that's guarding you gets kicked out, it means that you knew how to position and move yourself, in order to put your defender in that position —and the team supported your efforts. Every penalty shot your team gets to take is the result of teamwork as well. If you get a new shot clock while on offense, it's again proof that the whole team worked as one. When these instances occur, the whole team should feel a silent good job for their effort, and start building the action again.

The reason that I listed all of these examples of teamwork is because often they are overlooked and not addressed by both players and coaches. All of the hard work that a team puts into practicing different drills over and over, and conditioning their bodies to be at peak performance, should translate into an almost effortless game in the water. The spectators have very little idea of how much concentration and skill it takes to achieve greatness. Only the coach and the players should know how difficult it really is to get to that point.

TWELVE WEEK, OFF-SEASON, STRENGTH BUILDING WATER POLO WORKOUT

This workout program is for students who have already hit puberty. It is designed to increase the body's muscle strength to both enhance player performance and prevent injury.

There are three mesocycles in the routine, which lasts a total of 12 weeks. I would suggest that this program be started during the off-season, so that the players have a chance to taper a bit before they get into important competition again.

Each week the athletes should work out every other day, with a day of rest in between. As with any exercise routine, the athlete must always consult her doctor to determine if she is ready and able to lift weights. She should also consider hiring a personal trainer to ensure her form is perfect to prevent injury. The athletes should always use caution and honestly evaluate the amount of weight she uses so that she remains a first-string player.

Before each workout, the athlete should warm up on the cardio equipment for 10 to 15 minutes and should stretch for 10 to 15 minutes after every workout. Both elements are important; warming up because they need to ease into the workout and not stress their bodies and possibly injure themselves. Stretching is vital because lifting weights causes muscle shortening, thus inhibiting flexibility. Stretching brings back that flexibility by stretching the muscle groups worked during the program.

For each mesocycle, I have suggested the amount of weight to be used in relation to 1RM, which stands for 1 repetition maximum. To determine 1RM, and therefore determine the relative weight that should be used during each mesocycle, before the beginning of each mesocycle the athlete should be tested by a trainer doing the exercises I suggested with the maximum weight they can push.

I have assumed that the athletes are novice to weight training and so the first mesocycle starts with a full body, low weight/moderate rep circuit training program just to condition the tendons and muscles what is coming next. It lasts for three weeks. The second mesocycle, which last six weeks, is more intense, isolating specific muscle groups and using higher weights. The final three week mesocycle is even more intense and focuses on developing force by having the athlete perform fewer repetitions with even higher amounts of weight.

WEEKS 1 - 3: CIRCUIT TRAINING

With this circuit training program, the goal is to do the whole workout twice, in sequence, (i.e., exercises 1 -12 then repeat - no rest) on each workout day. The same exercises are done every workout for three weeks, so I have collapsed all three days into one grid for this mesocycle.

Circuit Training			
Days 1, 3 and 5 - Weeks 1 – 3			
Cardio Warm Up: 10 to 15 minutes			
Muscles Involved: Whole Body			
Weight Used: moderate 50% of your max capacity (1 RM)			
Exercise	**Reps**	**Weight**	**Sets**
1 Crunches	20 to 25		1
2 Side Planks	1 min		1
3 Back extension	10 to 15		1
4 Pull Ups	maximum #		1
5 Shoulder Front Raises	10 to 12		1
6 Squats	10 to 15		1
7 Biceps Curls	10 to 12		1
8 Triceps Cable Pull	10 to 12		1
9 Shoulder Lateral Raises	10 to 12		1
10 Rotator Cuff Band Inward Pull	10 to 12		1
11 Rotator Cuff Band Outward Pull	10 to 12		1
12 Flat Bench Press	10 to 12		1

WEEKS 4 - 9: HYPERTROPHY-INDUCING WORKOUT

For this mesocycle, I want the athlete to do three sets for each exercise and rest one minute between each set. This is a six week long cycle, and so I want the athlete to really push herself to build muscle mass and strength.

Hypertrophy-Inducing Workout			
Day 1, Weeks 4 – 9			
Cardio Warm Up - 10 to 15 minutes			
Muscles Involved: Core, Chest, Biceps, Rotator Cuff			
Weight Used: moderate to high; 70% of max capacity (1 RM)			
Exercise	Reps	Weight	Sets
1 Plank **a1***	1 min		3
2 Side Bends **a2**	10 to 15		3
3 Back extension **a3**	10 to 15		3
4 Flat Bench Press	8 to 10		3
5 Incline Dumbbell Press	8 to 10		3
6 Cable Chest Flies	10 to 12		3
7 Straight Bar Curls	10 to 12		3
8 Preacher Curls	10 to 12		3
9 EZ Bar Biceps Curls	10 to 12		3
a1, a2 and a3 are done consecutively three times through			

	Hypertrophy-Inducing Workout		
	Day 3, Weeks 4 – 9			
	Cardio Warm Up - 10 to 15 minutes			
	Muscles Involved: Core, Back, Triceps, Rotator Cuff			
	Weight Used: moderate to high; 70% of max capacity (1 RM)			
	Exercise	**Reps**	**Weight**	**Sets**
1	Russian Twist **a1***	10 to 15		3
2	Decline Crunches **a2**	10 to 15		3
3	Back Extension **a3**	10 to 15		3
4	Pull ups	max #		3
5	Bent over Dumbbell Row	10 to 15		3
6	Triceps Cable Pulldowns	10 to 12		3
7	Lying Triceps Extension	10 to 12		3
8	Rotator Cuff Internal Rotation Cable Pull	10 to 15	(low)	3
9	Rotator Cuff External Rotation Cable Pull	10 to 15	(low)	3

Hypertrophy-Inducing Workout			
Day 5, Weeks 4 – 9			
Cardio Warm Up - 10 to 15 minutes			
Muscles Involved: Core, Legs, Shoulders, Rotator Cuff			
Weight Used: moderate to high; 70% of max capacity (1 RM)			
Exercise	Reps	Weight	Sets
1 T Push up **a1***	10 to 15		3
2 Leg Raises **a2**	10 to 15		3
3 Back Extension **a3**	10 to 15		3
4 Leg Extensions	10 to 15		3
5 Hamstring Curls	10 to 15		3
6 Leg Press	10 to 15		3
7 Lateral Raises	8 to 10		3
8 Dumbbell Shoulder Press	8 to 12		3
9 Rotator Cuff External Rotation Cable Pull	10 to 15	(low)	3
10 Rotator Cuff Internal Rotation Cable pull	10 to 15	(low)	3

WEEKS 10 - 12: FORCE DEVELOPMENT PROGRAM

Do the number of sets listed, rest 2minutes between each set. For this mesocycle, the goal is to increase maximum force and to expose the athlete to more intense weight training. After this mesocycle, you can either go into tapering or you can create one more mesocycle where the athlete lifts heavier weights with fewer reps, closer to the 1 RM.

Force Development Program Day 1, Weeks 10 – 12			
Cardio Warm Up - 10 to 15 minutes			
Muscles Involved: Core, Chest, Back, Trapezius			
Weight Used: high; 80% of max capacity (1 RM)			
Exercise	**Reps**	**Weight**	**Sets**
1 Side Plank with Dip **a1***	8 to 10		3
2 Prone Leg Lifts **a2**	8 to 10		3
3 Supine Leg Lifts **a3**	8 to 10		3
4 Incline Barbell Press	5 to 8		3
5 Flat Dumbbell Press	5 to 8		3
6 Flat Dumbbell Fly	5 to 8		3
7 Lat Pull Down	5 to 8		3
8 Bent Over Barbell Row	5 to 8		3
9 Seated Low Row	5 to 8		3
10 Barbell Shrug	5 to 8		3
11 Deadlift	5 to 8		4
12 Stiff Leg Deadlift	5 to 8		3
a1, a2 and a3 are done consecutively three times through			

Force Development Program			
Day 3, Weeks 10 – 12			

Cardio Warm Up - 10 to 15 minutes

Muscles Involved: Core, Triceps, Biceps, Forearm, Rotator Cuff

Weight Used: high; 80% of max capacity (1 RM)

	Exercise	Reps	Weight	Sets
1	Swiss Ball Crunches **a1**	10 to 15		3
2	Supine Leg Raises on the Bench **a2**	10 to 15		3
3	Back Extension **a3**	10 to 15		3
4	Skull Crushers	5 to 8		3
5	Dips	8 to 10		3
6	Cable Curls	5 to 8		3
7	Straight Bar Biceps Curls	5 to 8		3
8	Preacher Curls	5 to 8		3
9	Underhand Grip Pull Ups	maximum #		3
10	Forearms Curls	5 to 8		3
11	Rotator Cuff Lying Dumbbell Internal Rotation	10 to 15	(low)	3
12	Rotator Cuff Lying Dumbbell External Rotation	10 to 15	(low)	3
	* a1, a2 and a3 are done consecutively three times through			

Force Development Program			
Day 5, Weeks 10 – 12			
Cardio Warm Up - 10 to 15 minutes			
Muscles Involved: Core, Quadriceps, Hamstrings, Calves, Rotator Cuff			
Weight Used: high; 80% of max capacity (1 RM)			
Exercise	**Reps**	**Weight**	**Sets**
1 Plank **a1**	10 to 15		3
2 Side Bends **a2**	10 to 15		3
3 Back Extension **a3**	10 to 15		3
4 Lunges	5-8		3
5 Platform Jumps	10 to 15	0	3
6 Calf Raises	5-8		3
7 Barbell Squats	5-8		3
8 Standing Calf Raises	10 to 15		3
9 Power Clean	10 to 12	(low)	
10 Rotator Cuff Internal Rotation Cable Pull	10 to 15	(low)	3
11 Rotator Cuff External Rotation Cable Pull	10 to 15	(low)	3

I am a firm believer in weight training in the development of the water polo player. While this program is designed for the athlete who has hit puberty, some form of strength training can be done for the pre-pubescent athlete as well. All of the dragging, pulling, pushing involved in competitive play requires a great deal of strength, so this training program will lay the groundwork for successful players.

A WORD ON NUTRITION

This is not meant to be a textbook on the way an athlete should eat, but I do want to say that I encourage my team to eat clean, eat green, eat lean. All athletes require a lot of calories to stay competitive, but these calories should be in the form of whole grains, lean protein, complex carbohydrates, and Omega 3 and Omega 6 rich fats.

The diet of an athlete and the diet of a teenager are often at direct odds. It's not easy to find a wide variety of healthy choices at the school cafeteria, though things seem to be changing in the US as even fast food restaurants offer apples instead of fries and have salads instead of chips. Preparing meals at home ahead of time is still, for now, the ultimate solution.

The diet will vary for gender, age, and amount of athletic activity, but as a general rule, healthy choices should be made by the athlete and supported by the family. I recommend that the serious water polo player consult a nutritionist and determine a meal plan for herself.

GLOSSARY OF TERMS

1. Set a pick: Collaboration of two players with a goal to open one or both of them from their defenders. Usually one player on offense positions herself so that the other player's defender cannot follow her player. This offensive tactic is utilized when the defense is playing pressure defense tactic.

2. Jumping zone defense: This type of defense consists of pressuring the player with the ball (because we don't want to allow that player has too much time to take a shot), while other defensive players are slightly backed up with their arms up blocking shots and paying attention that the hole-man doesn't get the ball. This tactic is used when we have a descent goalie who can stop most of the outside shots.

3. Shallow zone defense: This type of defense consists of totally taking the hole-man out of equation, with the whole team sloughing, except the center-defender (player #6) who is behind his player. Here we are allowing the outside players to take the shots at their will, and all we are doing for defense is trying to block those shots when they are taken. This tactic is used when we have a great goalie who can stop a vast majority of the outside shots.

4. M-zone defense: This type of defense neutralizes the center player completely by positioning a top driver defender in front of the center, while the two side players are positioned in between the three outside players. Good for producing counterattacks, this defense can be dangerous if there are good shooters in offensive positions #2, 3 or 4.

5. Combined zone defense: This type of defense has elements of jumping and shallow zone defense. For certain players the defense will pressure and attack them when they are in possession of the ball, but on some players they will not. Instead of attacking the player with the ball, certain players will remain back in front of the center blocking the shots, and preventing the ball to be passed into the center. Usually during the game analysis and before the match, the coach will determine which players will be guarded and which can be let shooting. In the figure bellow, we have defensive players 2 & 3 playing jumping zone defense, while players 1, 4 & 5 play shallow zone defense.

6. Sculling: the movement of one or both arms in order to stay above the surface of the water or to get as high up as possible. In order to get high above the water sculling is used together with the eggbeater. Sculling is used when field players are blocking the shot: they have one arm up – blocking the shot, one arm sculling – getting high above the water, eggbeater kick – getting high above the water and moving in desired direction.

Sculling is also used by the goalies for the same reason – to get up high with their bodies right before they go for the jump and make a save.

7. Goal line: the line on which the goals float, which extends from one post to the outer corner of the pool, also called the out of bounds line. This line is not only a line in between two posts, but also a line that goes from one post to the out of bounds line.

8. Rear Back (RB): This technique consists of a player driving toward the goal and suddenly changing direction by throwing herself on her back. The defender will not know when the player is going to change direction and will continue swimming towards the cage. This late realization will result in the player getting open.

9. Tapering: The practice of reducing exercise in the period that leads up to an important competition.

10. Mesocycle: In sports periodization, we have macrocycles, mesocycles and microcycles to ramp up the body and avoid "plateauing" and hitting the ceiling in training. This is an excellent way to train for competitions; planning a routine with exercises that build on each other. One mesocycle is a phase of training, usually lasting from two weeks up to six weeks, in which you stick to a specific routine.

SECRETS OF A SERBIAN WATER POLO COACH:
TABLE OF FIGURES

23043297R00075

Made in the USA
San Bernardino, CA
19 January 2019